"Stefan, when I think of you I'm reminded of the words from the late Benjamin Disraeli: 'Every production of genius must be the production of enthusiasm.' You inspire and motivate others to take their lives to a higher level."

Dave LaRue, Entrepreneur and CEO, Baldwin Supply Co.

"As the chief executive of a 10-year-old, Chicago-based digital agency, I have had the pleasure of working with brilliant entrepreneurs, established companies, and household brand names. It is not often that I come across a person who inspires such positive change both professionally and personally in my life. Stefan offers an honest, transparent approach to business and his overwhelming desire to truly leave a person better than when he first met them is a testament to his character. Thank you, Stefan."

Todd Brook, CEO, envisionit media

"Stefan Wissenbach has created an extraordinarily simple and powerful 21st-century solution for millions of individuals and for the whole world. I was instantly inspired and transformed when he first told me about his Magic Future vision and the Magic Number capability that everybody can master in a matter of a few minutes. Strategic Coach is proud to have been the first business to provide its entire staff with Magic Future as a benefit. I think it's a great innovation and I'm telling everyone I know about it."

Dan Sullivan, Strategic Coach

"Since the first day I met Stefan I have been impressed with the success he has created in his life as a successful entrepreneur [and] most of all, his impeccable character, his infectious charisma, and the feeling of total positive focus he gives to everyone he meets from the bellman to the company president."

Vic Conant, Chairman of the Board, Nightingale-Conant Corp

"I regard Stefan as a unique, talented, and visionary entrepreneur. His approach to simplifying the complex and creating Magicfuture.com is simply inspiring. Hundreds of thousands, if not millions of individuals will have their futures enhanced by the tools and capabilities that he has created. Stefan, I salute you for your vision, your application, and for the difference you will make in the world."

Mark Westcott, CEO, Strategic Evolution Pty, Australia

"*Slaying Dragons and Moving Mountains* is really an inspiration and kick-start for me to find meaningful perspective in my life and realize that I, too, can have the type of existence people often only dream of. Sometimes it takes having someone with experience to motivate and break it down for you to see that small actions can lead to large outcomes, and that's exactly what Stefan does in his book—makes greatness feel attainable. And I'm now successfully inspired to put an action plan together for a future I can, and already do, feel really excited about."

Marissa Liesenfelt, Senior Project Manager, envisionit media

Slaying Dragons and Moving Mountains

The MAGIC Formula for a happy, fulfilled life...

STEFAN WISSENBACH

For information on special sales and bulk purchases of this
book, please contact Inquiries@StefanWissenbach.com.

Published by Stefan Wissenbach, LLP

Publishing services by Social Motion Publishing
Mona Kuljurgis, editor; Melissa Schmidt, designer
SocialMotionPublishing.com

Second Print Edition

Produced and Printed in The United States of America

To my "community": thank you.

Contents

Important!

To get the full value from this book and maximize your success, go to:

StefanWissenbach.com/SDMMbonus

There, you can download the accompanying workbook as well as gain complimentary access for 3 months to MagicFuture.com, which provides many valuable tools to help you implement the MAGIC Formula.

Introduction

A FLYING BROOM. WHITE SPARKS EMITTED from a wand. A cloak that makes you invisible. For as long as I can remember, I've been fascinated by magic: wizards, witches, magicians, and the magical worlds they live in—creatures imbued with special powers that defy natural laws and make the impossible possible.

Most of us have dreamt of possessing supernatural abilities, the power to flick a wand, wave a hand, or whoosh a cloak to transform our very ordinary lives into extraordinary ones. But here's the thing: Performing a magic trick in real life doesn't actually involve any magic—and neither does living a rewarding, fulfilled, magical life.

It only looks like it does.

From a very young age, I often wondered why it is that so many people live lives of quiet desperation and unfulfilled potential, when a small number seem to perform their own magic and live fun, abundant, inspiring lives.

Is it magic?

No. A master magician hones his craft with skill, technique, knowledge, and practice, and pulls off what looks like the miraculous.

Living a great life is no different.

Magic is wonderful. It normally has a great outcome. As children, we're fascinated by magic and the art of the possible—because we haven't been told it's impossible. But, as we grow up, we are often made to feel that life should be far less exciting than the magical tales we were told as children.

And I think that's wrong.

Life can be magical, and I'd like to show you how. Making magic in real life is about mastery, not mystery—mastery of a way of doing things that creates an exceptional outcome. To the outside world, it'll look like you've performed the impossible. And that's really fun!

As children, we donned our capes, brandished our swords, and climbed imaginary mountains to slay powerful dragons. Then, as adults, our imaginary mountains and dragons turned into real aspirations and obstacles. But commitments, obligations, and daily-life tedium often chip away at our happiness and motivation, causing our goals and dreams to appear unreachable. As a result, too many of us no longer believe we can slay dragons or move mountains.

And I think that's wrong too!

As you'll discover in the pages ahead, I've developed a modern-day "MAGIC Formula." Mastering it will enable you to slay your own dragons—those things holding you back—and move your own mountains—achieve those big goals and important dreams in your life. Whether those take you around the world and back again, or just take place in your own backyard, it doesn't matter. What's important is that your mountains represent things that are meaningful to you—things which, when achieved, will give you a wonderful sense of fulfillment. And those pesky dragons you'll slay will empower you to progress and be happier.

As you'll discover in the pages ahead, I've developed a modern-day "MAGIC Formula."

A Wonderful Lifestyle

Today, I enjoy a very comfortable lifestyle. I have a large country property—with staff—and travel all over the world with my fabulous wife and three delightful children. I've enjoyed staying in many fine hotels, experienced different cultures, learned to snowboard, fly helicopters, and am able to indulge a passion for sports cars.

But that was not always the case.

My childhood was happy, but I grew up in a small apartment with my mother, sister, and hardly any money. I was nicknamed "lentil boy" at school because my mother bought and soaked lentils as a cheap way of feeding my sister and me. I left school early because I wanted to create my own financial independence and achieve my own goals. But, despite all this, I never saw a limit to my own potential. I still don't. And yet, as I look around me, I see so many wonderful people who have put a ceiling on theirs.

A Story About Fleas

A number of years ago, I was told this story: Some fleas were put in a glass, and as you would expect, immediately proceeded to jump out. They were put back in and, to prevent them from jumping out again, a lid was placed on the glass so every time they jumped they came up against the lid. After jumping and hitting the lid many times, they started to jump so that their spring took them just below the lid. And so they carried on jumping, not hitting the lid any longer. After a while the lid was removed. The fleas, now conditioned to springing only so high, continued to do so despite the fact there was nothing stopping them from jumping higher and escaping.

I often meet people just like these fleas. They've been told they can't do this, they can't do that, and as a result, have adopted the mindset that higher levels of success can only be achieved by other people.

Their experiences, the people they've mixed with, and the things they've been told have made them think that there's a lid on how high they can jump. The reality is, there isn't. The world is full of people who have not adopted the flea mentality and who are achieving great things. I want *you* to be one of them!

That said, success rarely happens by accident.

In my case, it's the result of significant personal investment, application, and learning. Still today, I continue to invest in my personal growth and development. I travel from England to Chicago every 90 days to meet my coach, Dan Sullivan. Since the age of 18, I have attended many personal development seminars, read dozens and dozens of books, and listened to hours of audio programs by inspirational thought-leaders. In fact, I'm almost always reading an account of someone's success story or a book on personal development—so much so that it's become a bit of a joke in my family!

We stand on the shoulders of giants, and I am eternally grateful to all those who share their wisdom to help make our lives better.

If you put the considerable time investment aside, I have conservatively invested well over $500,000 in my development over the years, and this figure continues to rise. I believe that each of us should invest in ourselves, and consider the price—in time and money—an *investment*, not a cost.

I totally appreciate that it's not practical for everyone to invest this sort of money or time. It's for this reason that I've written this book, to share with you the skills, techniques, and knowledge that you need to create what will appear to be your own magic. Much of it is uncommon common sense. It is not a detailed academic study or a work of literary excellence. I'm pretty down to earth, and so is this book.

Contained within these pages are what I consider to be the best bits—the bits that work—which I've verified in over 20 years of learning and investment. I've stripped out the jargon and the fluff, as I've found people crave simplicity.

There's a lot of information available to help people become more successful, but it's often too complex. I like things to be simple—and I'm good at simplifying complexity—so I've distilled what I've learned into the MAGIC Formula I spoke of earlier. I've personally used it to great effect, have shared it with my children, and have used it to improve the lives of others. I am living proof that it works!

I Need You to Think

I want this book to make you think. I don't want you to wait until it's too late to start thinking, because thinking is healthy! I've noticed over the years how so many people get stuck in a routine or way of life, to the extent that they sometimes stop thinking about what could be or how they could improve their lives. They go day to day, seldom giving any meaningful thought to their futures.

Not thinking about the future is very dangerous. It's less dangerous if you are fortunate enough to have guaranteed income for life—and even then it's a shame, because not thinking about the future means you are unlikely to fulfill your potential, which I think is tragic.

Many people put their heads in the sand and hope that it will all come good one day.

I love to see people fulfill their potential. Many people are frightened to think about the future, as it often feels too big an issue to tackle. The thought of becoming too old to work—or retiring with no money—is unpalatable, and often too uncomfortable to think about. Many people put their heads in the sand and hope that it will all come good one day.

For most it won't.

The only way to improve your situation is to *take control.* The first step is to start *thinking*. It costs nothing, and while it may prove a little uncomfortable initially, most fears, when faced, disappear. When you begin to think about your situation—where you are, where you'd like to be—there's often a magic that starts to work and you begin to build momentum. You're able to make smarter decisions and identify ways that you previously might have missed to help you get to where you want to be.

It's energizing and uplifting when you change your life for the better. Change takes time, and many people leave thinking until it's too late.

I was talking to my brilliant assistant, Jayne, about how this book and my website, MagicFuture.com, help people *think* about the future. She told me about an experience she had several years ago in the grocery store: Perusing the aisles, she saw an older woman nearby and noticed she was buying poor-quality, cheap food. Striking up a conversation with her in the checkout line, the 83-year-old woman said that she was going out to work as a cleaner that evening, because her pension didn't go far enough. Jayne was horrified. While she felt sorry for the woman, she vowed at that moment to take control of her own life to avoid being in anything like a similar situation in many years to come. It's a great reminder that the time for taking control is now.

Pain Weighs Ounces, and Regret Weighs Tons

It may initially feel painful to do some thinking about the future, but it will certainly enable you to avoid the regret that results from doing nothing. What's more, the energy you get from taking control will certainly help you achieve more and love life!

Most people are living busy lives and neglecting the most important person in the world—themselves! People today are busy working, building their careers or businesses, and often find themselves playing catch-up with a variety of tasks. Outside of work, their time is spent juggling other priorities, so it's little wonder that with whatever little time is left, they tend to switch off, rather than switching on, to build a brighter future (or even a magic one!). In today's fast-paced world, people are often so busy that they seldom take time out for themselves. And by time for themselves, I mean time to learn and reflect, develop new skills, grow, and plan for a brighter, bigger, and better future.

People frequently put others' needs ahead of their own and often find themselves at the end of a very long line. They believe they're working hard today for a better tomorrow—and as a result, working hard *now* is what they focus on. They frequently put things off, but when we're always consumed with today, tomorrow never comes.

The MAGIC Formula I will share with you has made, and continues to make, a tremendous difference in my life. The formula is timeless; successful people have used it for centuries.

I really want the rest of your life to be the best of your life! I know that if you are committed to the same goal, great things will happen. Happily ever after needn't just exist in fairy tales. This book will show you how you can make it come true for you.

The MAGIC Formula I will share with you has made, and continues to make, a tremendous difference in my life. The formula is timeless; successful people have used it for centuries. It is also my hope that you will read it again and again in the future, as your life develops and changes, so you continue to get value and insights to help you progress even further.

So, do you want to make positive changes in your life, be happier, and be in a position one day where work is optional? It's not a trick question. While it's easy to answer "yes" (indeed, it would sound pretty silly to answer "no"), change only happens when change happens. In other words, if you keep on doing what you've always done, you'll get what you've always gotten.

To help you implement change, included in each chapter are practical exercises that will help to fortify the insights you gained from the text. Complete these exercises sequentially, and permit them to build upon one another. Also, feel free to take breaks to allow yourself to become familiar with new changes. Not only will these exercises reinforce the knowledge you've gained from this book, each exercise will move you one step closer to completing a blueprint-type document that has worked magic in my own life, as I believe it will work in yours.

Magic Action

Be sure to download your copy of the interactive workbook that contains all the exercises in this book. Go to StefanWissenbach.com/SDMMbonus for immediate access.

Uncharted Territory

Few would dream of striking out on a journey through uncharted territory without a map. Even Lewis and Clark, the early nineteenth-century explorers who charted the American northwest, took Sacagawea along as a guide. Yet, so many of us strike out on life's journey with little guidance and without a clear vision of where we'd like to go or how we'd like to get there.

For many years, I have carried around a document in my pocket that I call my Magic Map. It is a detailed outline of the goals, milestones, and habits I'd like to acquire, and the dates by which I'd like to acquire them. Over time, it has served as inspiration, information, and motivation, and has kept me on track—even through the rough times. It will for you too. If you visit my website, StefanWissenbach.com, you can download your own Magic Map. As you make your way through the book and each of the exercises, fill in your Magic Map with your own dates, goals, and achievements. By the time you finish this book, you'll have a fully complete Magic Map, providing clarity on what you want your life to look like—and, most importantly, a route to get there. Print yours out and keep it in your pocket, as I have. Or post it on your office wall or next to your mirror. Take a look at your Magic Map as often as possible, but especially when you're feeling discouraged. It will serve as a beacon and a guide on your journey through unfamiliar terrain.

> You owe it not only to yourself to chart your own course and set your own path, but to those who came before you who fought so hard to grant you the opportunity to do so.

And one more word about unfamiliar terrain. Now that we're in the second decade of the twenty-first century, it's important to look back on the territory from which we came. At one time, it was true that being born to a certain station in life sealed your fate—being born female, into poverty, or of a certain race or religion directed the course of your life for the rest of your life. But so many have fought for so long to have those barriers lifted. And after years of perseverance, many of the barriers have been removed—removed for you! So, you owe it not only to yourself to chart your own course and set your own path, but to those who came before you who fought so hard to grant you the opportunity to do so. You are their legacy. Do right by them.

Confidence is Low

At the time of this writing, public confidence is very low. There's a lack of trust in politicians, in government, and in the financial institutions that people rely on for secure futures. Many people are feeling vulnerable. I sympathize and understand why so many people feel trapped, not knowing which way to turn. However, I also passionately believe the only way to change your life for the better is to take control, ownership, and responsibility. Many people go about blaming society, government, or the economic climate for their current situation. While these things clearly have an impact, it's within the power of each and every one of us to individually take control and make things better. Peter Haddon, my first coach, used to say, "When you point the finger, look at your hand, and you'll see there are three fingers pointing back at you."

Give yourself a little space and think.

Opportunity is nowhere.

Read it again.

Now read this:

Opportunity is now here.

See what a difference a little space makes!

Despite the economic downturn, it's still a great time to be building a brighter future. We are living in a wonderful time of rapid technological innovation and progress, which is causing the world to change at an enormous rate. There are opportunities everywhere.

I've written this book because the time is now to focus on changing your life for the better, and because I've noticed that so many people are tired of the same routine—slave, save, retire, exist, and then run out of time! So many now question this routine as they feel *there just absolutely has to be more to life.*

Happiness and fun are what life is all about, and I'm also convinced you learn more when having fun. If you're not, it can have a negative impact, as it's taking up time when you could be having fun. That is my primary goal for you in reading this book—and ultimately for your life!

Gandhi once said, "Live every day as if it were your last, but plan as if you were going to live forever." It seems like a contradiction, and very much a tall order, yet it's a quote I've had on my office wall for many years. You may have heard phrases such as "you only live once," "life is not a rehearsal," and "success is a journey not a destination." I subscribe to them all, but in the end, for me, life is about learning and having fun. That is what this book is all about and, ultimately, what the MAGIC Formula is for. So let's learn a little, have some fun, and move you toward the life you truly desire.

How to Get the Most Out of This Book

I really want you to get the most out of this book. In order for you to do so, here are some steps. Follow these just like a magician performs a trick, exactly in the right order, and you'll create your own magic.

1. Minds are like parachutes—most useful when open. Be open-minded and suspend disbelief, because what's in this book works. The principles, techniques, and lessons you will learn have been tried and tested over many years. I have used them personally and can attest to their effectiveness.

2. Don't be misled by the simplicity. Some of what I say will be obvious to you, and some of it will seem really simple. Don't let this put you off. Success is simple disciplines practiced daily, and the difference between an ordinary person and an *extra*ordinary one is just that little *extra*. If you are already doing everything in this book, I applaud you—you certainly don't need my help! But, in my experience, even successful people often don't do the simple things that would make them even more successful. Why is this? I've asked myself this question many times. I think it's because we get put off by the simplicity and think that greatness will only come through greater complexity. After over 20 years, I've found no evidence that this is true. So, I urge you, don't be put off by the simplicity.

3. Think of this book like a jigsaw puzzle. Normally, when you put a puzzle together, you have the finished picture to help you. In this case, however, there is no picture. *When* this all starts to come together for you will depend on who you are. For some readers, it will happen early, and for others it will happen at the very end of the book, when you have completed your Magic Map. Don't worry about when it comes together, it will—and when is not important. Also, don't be daunted if you get lots of new information and insight. I'll be showing you how to implement the learning in a calm, efficient manner as you move forward. You don't immediately have to implement all the insights; the important thing is that they are captured in the first place.

4. Read with a pen. Think about the words—and don't rush. As you read things that resonate with you and provide you with a-ha moments, take the pen and mark the page. Capture your insights and make them your own. The more you personalize your book, the greater your ownership will be. I've deliberately left plenty of space on each page for your notes.

5. Complete the exercises! Throughout this book, you

will be prompted to capture insights or complete an exercise relevant to what you have just read. I ask for your trust. If there's an exercise to do, it's because I believe it will make a difference. Completing these will do several things:

First, it will provide you with additional insight. I find time and again that when my coach asks me to complete an exercise, doing so deepens my learning and fortifies my new thoughts and understanding.

Second, each and every exercise is designed to deliver a specific output, which will help you build a robust context, framework, and plan to reinforce what you've learned.

Third, the exercises will provide you with the ability to translate what you've learned into an action plan, and action plans translate into meaningful results.

Last, if the exercise asks you to transfer the end result to your Magic Map, *please do it.* Don't wait until later. Your Magic Map should be built as you make your way through the book.

6. Tell the truth. It's so important to tell the truth! Not only is the truth easier to remember, but all progress starts with telling the truth. You are where you are, and you know where you are. Don't fight it—embrace it. Be truthful, and you can then truly begin the process of making lasting positive change. Remember, what you're thinking and writing down is entirely personal to you. It's up to you whether to share it with anyone or not.

7. Accept that things have to change. That you've read this far is very promising! Remember, "Do what you've always done and you'll get what you've always gotten." The only way to change your outcomes is if you change your behaviors. Don't be frightened of change. This is not a book you just read. I am going to ask you to take action regularly throughout. If you want to change your life for the better, you need to take action. We live in a changing world, and being someone who embraces change and continuously seeks to improve is an empowering way to live. If you don't change as the world changes, you'll be left behind.

8. Don't try to do it all at once. Trying to change lots of things at once increases risk of failure. Instead, make and master small changes—one or two at a time. You may want to pause in your reading to let some changes sink in, and enjoy their benefits, before picking up the book again and moving onto the next phase. Go at a pace that suits you—and remember to enjoy the experience!

9. Please do implement the insights. To some readers this will be obvious, but I'm going to make a point of stating it. I've known many people who have read books and attended seminars, courses, and workshops. They get some great insights but then don't implement anything. All that happens is that they get a short-term burst of motivation, but ultimately there's no application. Without application, there's no growth. If you read this book and nothing changes, it will be because you haven't implemented the insights—and it will have been a waste of your time. Please don't do this. I want you to be happier and in a better place than when you started. Implement the insights!

10. Read with a smile! Changing your life for the better should be fun. We all learn more when we're having fun!

Now, let's cover the first FUNdamental—your *happiness.*

Happiness

The late Stephen Covey, in his critically acclaimed, best-selling book *The Seven Habits of Highly Effective People,* listed the first habit as "begin with the end in mind." So, the first thing I want to spend some time with you on is the ultimate goal—your happiness.

What would make you happier? More money? More free time? Better relationships? A new job? Better health?

The dictionary defines happiness as something that results from the possession or attainment of what one considers good—in other words, your achieving what matters to you.

I passionately believe that for each and every one of us, our personal level of happiness is the most important thing.

Why do I say this? Well, I think that happiness is, frankly, life's driving force.

Everything we do in life either adds to or takes away from our level of happiness. Everything we aspire to achieve or acquire is done so in the belief that it will make us happier. Where we have a choice to do something that makes us happy, rather than unhappy, we'll often choose the happy route. In a great relationship? Happy. In bad relationship? Unhappy. Enjoying work? Happy. Dislike what you do for a living? Unhappy. You get the picture.

When I look at all of my aspirations, goals, and achievements, they all positively impacted my level of happiness. However, sometimes on the route to greater happiness, you do need to make some short-term sacrifices that, on their own, may not make you happy—but you do so because they will *ultimately* make you happier. After all, why strive to do something that makes you unhappy unless it leads to substantially greater happiness?

Think about things you are doing right now in your life that don't make you happy. Write them down. Check that each and every one of them has the *potential* to deliver substantially greater happiness in the future. If they don't, think very carefully about whether you should be doing them at all!

Magic Action

Complete Magic Action #1 in your workbook: "What Doesn't Make You Happy."

When you are aware of what you need to do to improve your levels of happiness, you've taken the first big step to achieving a life of fulfillment.

Having spent over 20 years providing strategic consultancy advice to private individuals, I've noticed a direct correlation between financial independence and happiness. One of the first things I always do with my clients is to help them understand their unique "Magic Number"—the amount of wealth they need so that work is optional. Why? Because having the resources to afford to *choose* whether or not to work has a big impact on your levels of happiness.

You can understand why: You don't have to do a job you don't enjoy, you have the freedom to pursue hobbies or interests that excite you and make you happy, you have less time pressure and can spend more time with loved ones. Later in this book, I'll explain how you can discover your own Magic Number.

You're only on this earth for a relatively short period of time, and it's really important that you enjoy it! I'm not just talking about bursts of happiness, such as enjoying a great night out with friends or spending quality time with a loved one; I'm talking about an ongoing state of happiness—feeling at peace.

Happiness is more about fulfillment and personal achievement than the acquisition of material things.

We all have basic needs that, if not fulfilled, make us unhappy. Our health is important, as is our ability to enjoy shelter and warmth. Beyond that, happiness becomes a very personal thing. The world is such a wonderful place; there are so many opportunities and experiences open to each and every one of us. There is a vast spectrum of choice to create happiness. However, it's fair to say that many people will perceive that their own lack of happiness often comes down to a lack of money.

Happiness is more about fulfillment and personal achievement than the acquisition of material things. Over the years, I have set many goals, and I continue to do so. As someone who has a passion for cars, one of the goals I set was to own a Ferrari before age 30, and a Rolls-Royce before age 40. I achieved both goals. But I got more pleasure from the *journey* to the goal than when the cars were actually delivered. While it's great to own nice things, it's quite often the sense of achievement and personal satisfaction you get from being in the *position* to buy something that gives the greatest sense of gratification and well-being. You should bear this in mind when you set about improving your life.

So, how do you measure and improve your levels of happiness?

Magic Action

Complete Magic Action #2 in your workbook: "The Magical Happiness Test."

It will help you define what makes you happy and what doesn't. When you have clarity on what makes you happy, you can then choose to spend more time on things that do and less time on things that don't. Once you've finished reading this book, I'll ask you to retake the happiness test and compare your score with the previous one. Then, retake the happiness test every 90 days—and compare results. It's worth doing this test just four times a year to ensure you're as happy as possible.

Unless you honestly feel that you are truly at the highest levels of happiness, you should be taking action on an ongoing basis to improve your happiness, and eliminate situations that make you unhappy.

Making Magic

Now that you've got a happiness benchmark, let's talk about how to maintain your position and move it forward.

I've spent many years working- with successful people while simultaneously studying the field of human development. During this time, I've discovered five key elements that comprise the bedrock of happiness and success. They are: **M**otivation, **A**pplication, **G**rowth, **I**ndependence, and **C**ommunity—**MAGIC**. Together, these principles promote the attainment of the peace and well-being we all desire.

Motivation. Many tasks that are very much worth doing—and end up with a bountiful payoff—don't generate immediate results. Improving your health starts imperceptibly, with daily changes in diet and exercise. Tackling debt requires financial restraint, discipline, and allocating money to areas that no longer bring instant gratification. Changing jobs requires incessant resumé submission, interviews, and much rejection. To maintain fortitude and stamina in all these areas requires motivation—and the energy and enthusiasm that it brings. Without motivation, getting started may look attractive, but keeping going will be tough. It fuels your momentum and forward movement, even when your energy is low and commitment waning. Stoking the fires of passion for your desired life will always bring that life within closer reach.

Application. In his noted book, *The War of Art*, Steven Pressfield asks, "Late at night have you experienced a vision of the person you might become, the work you could accomplish, the realized being you were meant to be? Are you a writer who doesn't write, a painter who doesn't paint, an entrepreneur who never starts a venture? Then you know what Resistance is." Pressfield defines the gulf between the motivation to achieve something and the actual achievement of it as *Resistance*, and the overcoming of Resistance as the singular objective in accomplishing any goal. It is an integral concept. So many people are mere students of change. Successful people get things done. You always need to physically start doing something, or you end up like so many individuals—filled with motivation but going nowhere. Follow-through is imperative. Once you've got motivation, you need to transfer that energy, enthusiasm, and passion into unbridled application.

Growth. The happy consequence of application and taking action is that you start to learn—and as you learn, you grow. Successful people learn from all their experiences, good and bad, and transfer that learning into growth and gaining better results. Growth is of fundamental importance. It is, in fact, the bedrock of the human experience itself, and indeed all life. Even the most sedentary living thing is in motion and experiencing constant change. As human beings, however, we have the ability to direct the course of our growth, and that is the entire intent behind the MAGIC Formula.

Independence. Why do we grow? What is all this motivation translated into application winding up in growth for? Why all the effort? It is for independence. Growth leads to freedom, independence, and the ability to choose the direction our lives will take. At this writing, many people are fighting and dying around the world for the chance at independence, for the opportunity to direct the course of their own lives. Financial freedom, even in small doses, magnifies that opportunity, and multiplies the options to choose what we want to do, and when we want to do it. Do you want to take a luxury vacation or a rustic one, obtain an advanced degree or start a business, devote your time to non-profit causes or travel the world, pay off the car or start an emergency fund? Financial freedom brings with it not only the obvious consumer perks, it permits you to be in control, personally and professionally, of your time, your efforts, and your destiny.

Community. Americans, in particular, have a fascination with individualism—the rugged cowboy conquering the West, the lone renegade seeking justice for the wronged. Though these caricatures make great movie roles, in truth, success is a more collaborative effort. Over the years, it has been my observation that happy and successful people operate in community. All of the top entrepreneurs, chief executives, and business owners I've worked with appreciate the power of community. Without it, you're on your own—and this will seriously limit your potential. Successful people rely on a network of supportive individuals they love and care about, with whom they can share their aspirations, goals, and achievements, and who provide feedback and encouragement on disappointments and setbacks—whether that community is blood-related or not. That's how it worked for me, and I'm sure that's how it will work for you, too. Life is meant to be shared, and not only is tackling any goal more difficult by yourself, it's just not as fun.

"Whatever you can do, or dream you can, begin it. Boldness has genius, magic, and power in it. Begin it now."
-Johann Von Goethe

And, there you have it! The five elements that make up my MAGIC Formula: Motivation, Application, Growth, Independence, and Community.

As you read on, we'll explore these in more detail, and I'll show you how to get the most from each. When you work these five concepts, you may be accused of conjuring up real magic, because the results can appear astounding. Still, as I mentioned at the beginning of this chapter, I like to think of my MAGIC Formula as a road to mastery, not miracles or mystery—mastery of a way of thinking, of key actions and applications, and a process that will profoundly impact your life. And, in the end, when you apply the MAGIC Formula to your life, you may find that a dose of *real* magic does find you after all. This should be expected. As we are reminded in the immortal words of Johann Von Goethe, "Whatever you can do, or dream you can, begin it. Boldness has genius, magic, and power in it. Begin it now."

Inspired? I hope so. This is only the beginning!

M

Motivation

"Be miserable. Or motivate yourself.
Whatever has to be done, it's always your choice."
DR. WAYNE DYER

MOTIVATION IS THE FIRST INGREDIENT in my MAGIC Formula. As we move closer to our Magic Numbers and bigger futures, the long and winding road to success is often blocked by huge mountains and fierce dragons. Slaying those dragons and moving those mountains demands grit, commitment, and perseverance. It requires understanding why you're embarking on this journey in the first place; it requires motivation.

Appreciation and Authenticity

My coach, Dan Sullivan, has a number of principles he likes

to convey to his clients, two of which I'd like to share with you here. They are:

- You can't have what you want until you want what you have.
- All progress starts with telling the truth.

These two principles, when considered genuinely, can instigate a tectonic shift in your life because, truth be told, they're so often the opposite of how we actually live our lives.

Each day, commercial messaging barrages us from all sides, demanding we be discontent with every facet of our existence, our house, our car, our clothes, our mate, even ourselves. In this environment, it's so difficult to extract who we really are from the noise, take a few steps back, gain perspective, and truly appreciate all the good that has come our way.

It is not always a default mode of thinking, but it is absolutely necessary if you're going to build on that good and make it grow.

The second adage, "all progress starts with telling the truth," can bring an even bigger seismic shift. Telling the truth, especially if it hasn't been a guiding principle so far, can dismantle every facet of your life like no other.

So many people have lost sight of where they are and find themselves living in denial. The same messaging that breeds so much discontent also berates anyone who doesn't conform to it, reviles failure, and overlooks the hard work and sustained focus needed in life to accomplish anything worthwhile.

Often, if our lives don't measure up to the commercial ideal, there can be a tendency to project the appearance they do anyway. This facade can become so unrelenting that we deceive not only others, but ourselves as well.

The key to my MAGIC Formula, however, is authenticity—the kind that arises from our most deeply held values and beliefs and results in genuine happiness and fulfillment. People who are truthful about themselves and their situations have a solid foundation to build upon. Knowing and owning where you are, before you strike out on your journey, is the first step to getting where you want to go!

So, understanding that "all progress starts with the truth" will help you set your compass and accurately plot out where you'd like to go. It's an invaluable precept that will guide your progress.

A good way to start incorporating these two principles into your life is to identify people you know (or have known) who exhibit appreciation and authenticity.

Complete Magic Action #3 in your workbook: "Appreciation and Authenticity."

Now, to keep you moving along, in the pages ahead I'm going to give you several practices that'll help you battle the monsters and move the granite along your road to success.

10 Magical Things About You

In 2011, I joined Joe Polish's "Genius Network" and have attended the meetings in Arizona regularly since. Joe is a brilliant marketer and connector who has a really fun and motivational way of explaining things. It was at my first meeting that he assigned an exercise that I value to this day. The exercise was to write down the ten coolest things about me. Now, even as an "open-minded Brit," as many Americans like to call me, the word "cool" didn't create a connection. As a father of three fabulous children, I do frequently get told how *uncool* I am. (Fashion sense, it appears, is reserved for those who have yet to learn how to properly wear pants....)

Anyhow, feeling a little self-conscious and somewhat stumped at first, I eventually gained some momentum, and the exercise became clear. The experience was very positive and made me feel grateful and appreciative for my qualities and where I currently am in my life.

On returning home to the United Kingdom, I asked my family to complete the exercise as well. Like me, they were a little hesitant at first, but became more confident as they wrote. It was absolutely fascinating to watch their reactions and energy change.

So often, we are taught to not be boastful, downplay our strengths, not appear arrogant, and even employ false modesty. However, we're all born with unique abilities and natural talents. To deny or downplay them robs not only you of the pleasure and satisfaction of engaging with and expressing them, it robs the world.

I've subsequently done this exercise with my team at work and other teams, always with similar results.

Now it's time for you to complete the MAGIC Formula version of this exercise, which I call "10 Magical Things About You." (Yes. I repurposed it. But Joe Polish is a wonderful guy, so it's with his permission!)

Before you do, here are a couple tips to keep it going smoothly:

- Many people feel self-conscious writing down what they're good at, but don't let that faze you. Persist with the exercise and your confidence and momentum will build.
- If you're so inspired, share your list with someone who knows you well. Third-party validation is a confidence booster, and your friend will undoubtedly come up with something you hadn't thought of. Better still, have them do the exercise about themselves!
- Remember, the only person the list is important to is *you*. It's only *your* opinion that matters, so don't let second-guessing or modesty dissuade you. If you think something's great or magical about you, it is. And don't just focus on the big stuff. When I first did this exercise with my family, my then-12-year-old son put near the top of his list his ability to make a brilliant chocolate cake, which he thinks is pretty cool. And, let me tell you, it's great cake!

Magic Action

Complete Magic Action #4 in your workbook: "10 Magical Things About You."

In case you're interested, here's my list as it was at the time we published this book.

Now, keep your "10 Magical Things About You" in front of your mind by entering your list onto your Magic Map. Know that, with time, your list will grow and change.

What's Really Important to You?

Now that we've got down some magical things about you, it's time to decipher what truly lights a fire in your gut—what's *really* important to you. Think about it. Most people go through life consumed by the day to day, seldom taking time to reflect on what is truly important to them. Lots of people I meet, many years into their careers, start to feel unhappy even though their careers and businesses are thriving. Fundamentally, the reason they're unhappy is that they have moved away from honoring what's vitally important to them.

Why do you need to know what's important to you? Well, it's key to the decisions you make about what to do, be, or have. Without this understanding, the emotional connection to follow through on your often long and winding road won't be there.

I've had the good fortune of working with many wealthy people over the last 25 years. Oftentimes, they have made lots and lots of money and achieved their Magic Numbers long ago. In some cases, however, when I look at their journeys, I see that they've come with failed marriages, missed time with their children, and a lack of quality friendships.

> It's important to have a balance between striving for financial independence and enjoying the things in life money can't buy.

As I've become close enough to speak frankly with these people, I've often asked: If they could, would they trade an element of their wealth today to recapture lost time with their children, friends, and relationships?

What do you think they say?

Almost without exception, they say yes.

Their replies have been very interesting to me. It proves, as I suspected, that life's *not* just about money, even in our money-centered culture. It's important to have a balance between striving for financial independence and enjoying the things in life money can't buy. This often takes discipline, as it's all too easy to become consumed by the pursuit of wealth.

People often confuse the size of their bank account with their own self-worth, for validation from those who've derided them in the past, or for vindication from some perceived wrong. They often feel that making even *more* money would make them happier, but frankly it can do the opposite.

Money is excellent for buying things, providing for those you love, and ensuring some security in this grueling, physical, and ever-changing world—but it is not a measure of your value on the planet, an indicator of your worth as a human being, or absolution for things you regret.

Those things are determined by your values and the actions you take to institute those values—and the money you make can work in the service of that, if you set about to use it that way.

But how do you identify what truly is important to you?

Here's an exercise I do with my clients:

Pause for a moment and imagine a large, softly lit, beautifully decorated room. Music is gently playing in the background. Looking around the room, you can see that it's full of your family, your friends, and associates past and present. There's that great hum of happy conversation in the room as people stand together, in groups, talking. You look around and, at the end of the room, see a big table. On the table is a box.

You are in the box!

Dead!

It's your funeral.

And it's a wonderful funeral—a celebration rather than a tragic affair. You've lived a long, successful, happy life and, having passed away peacefully in your sleep with no regrets, everyone has gathered to pay tribute to you and honor the life you've lived. And in this magical scenario, you can walk around the room and hear what is being said about you.

What would you like to hear? What would you like your friends, family, and colleagues to be saying about you? When finally reaching the end of your life, how would you like to be remembered, what impact would you like to have had, and what legacy would you like to leave? Perhaps there are certain people you would like to spend more time with, or things you've always wanted to do. We're all headed for that casket, sooner or later. There is very little hope of having a different past, but an immense amount of hope of having a different future. Let this moment move you to make that future one you truly desire.

Complete Magic Action #5 in your workbook: "What's Really Important?"

Once you've done this exercise, pause and reflect. What action could you take as a result? Then, consider adding this to your Magic Map.

So, What's Your Question?

Now that you have a bit of clarity on what's important to you, let's put the rubber to the road to transform those values into a focused query that lays out your intention.

My friend and mentor, Dave Larue, once asked me, "What's your question?" He explained that creating your own unique question is a great way to drill down your values and priorities into a concise query that narrows your focus and helps you zero in on what's most important to you. It allows you to better identify situations and opportunities that are in harmony with what you're trying to achieve.

When I first started work as a young man, my question was very straightforward: "How can I make enough money to support myself financially so I can leave home?"

Over time, this progressed to, "How can I best support my family and be a great husband, father, and friend?"

And through many changes, it has evolved to what it is today: "How can I help millions of people, while achieving all my goals and having a tremendous amount of fun along the way?"

It's a big question, and it has led me to launch the site MagicFuture.com. My business has come a long way since the idea came to me in 2008, and we've slain many dragons and moved many mountains along the way—all helped by the power of one question.

So think about yours.

What's the question you would like answered that would improve your life and/or the lives of others? Think about the previous exercise and what *truly* matters to your life right now? Don't overanalyze it. Write it down, knowing that it will change over time.

Starting your day with this important question is a powerful way to get your subconscious mind to work for you.

Format your question in this way:

"How can I ____________ while ____________?"

(The "while" part is recommended, but not required.)

A few examples are:

- How can I build a successful career while balancing the other priorities in my life?
- How can I start my new business while still supporting my living costs and family?
- How can I land a job I really enjoy while generating enough money to support myself?
- How can I turn my hobby and passion into my work?

Magic Action

Complete Magic Action #6 in your workbook: "What's Your Question?"

Starting your day with this important question is a powerful way to get your subconscious mind to work for you. After asking yourself the same question several times—an easy habit to adopt—you'll be amazed at how many opportunities present themselves that have the potential to provide the answer.

Now, enter your question into the designated area on your Magic Map. Look at it everyday, and let it motivate you to start moving your life into direction that matters most.

Discover Your Magic Number

Now, I'd like to spend some time helping you to understand your unique Magic Number and the importance of being in a position where, one day, work is optional. I passionately believe that each and every one of us wants to be in this position, and the sooner the better. It doesn't mean that we will necessarily stop work or no longer contribute to the greater good—it simply means we will have the choice to continue with our income-producing careers or not.

In my experience, people who've already achieved their Magic Numbers often go on to do their best work yet, unencumbered by financial obligations. They can focus their talents and abilities on advancing their highest values and priorities.

Rather than that day being close to the day we draw our last breath, you can bring that day sooner.

And of course, it's not *all* about amassing lots and lots of money—I firmly believe that quality of life is more important than quantity of money. But money is such a huge component of life's quality that engaging in a discussion about it without addressing money is virtually pointless and futile.

Even if you are not money motivated, and many people aren't, unless you live off the land scavenging for food and shelter, a decent existence in society requires some money—money to feed, clothe, shelter, and care for yourself in a way you would like.

So, if you are of the notion that money is ignoble, base, or lowly, know that you are doing a disservice to the things you most care about. Money can serve the highest instincts of humankind in the same way it can sabotage and debase them. It is the manner in which its power is wielded that makes the difference, and the manner in which that power is wielded is up to you.

DEAD ENDS AND SURVIVAL MODE

I would like to say a few words about dead-end jobs and the millions of people around the world earning menial wages. If you are a fast-food worker, a big-box retail clerk, a night watchman, you may think: I will never reach my Magic Number, not in a thousand lifetimes.

There are many dead-end jobs in the world that pay below a living wage. But because those *jobs* are dead-end does not mean *you* are. In the later chapter on Growth, you will find an array of options to update your skills that will help you earn a higher income, all without a hefty price tag or going back to school. There are also many well-earning trades and vocations that require only apprenticeships, not schooling. And lastly, many entrepreneurial ventures can be launched without any academic credential. In other words, if you are a retail clerk today, it does not mean you have to be a retail clerk tomorrow.

Know that a life of constant stress, crisis, and urgency can become an addiction.

Lastly, let's have a look at survival mode. Many of us have lived in survival mode and continue to do so; for some it is a fact of life, yet for some, it is a force of habit.

Besides the obvious practical difficulties of living hand to mouth, there can be something far more sinister and insidious about this mode of living. Survival mode is not only taxing and stressful, it can be an intense adrenaline rush, a life filled with direction and purpose and urgency. Survival mode can be high drama, with lows and highs that seem like you're really squeezing the most out of life.

When you're always one step shy of eviction, your mission is quite clear. Surviving preoccupies your time so that you never need to ask the bigger questions, like what's really important to you or how you'd like to be remembered. When you're working to keep the lights on and the rent paid, you know what you must do every day—you don't have to confront the discomfort of uncertainty, risk, and change.

Living in survival mode is also a sympathetic condition that can fuel the false benefits of victimhood, martyrdom, and self-sacrifice.

Certainly, not everyone living paycheck to paycheck qualifies for this description, but know that a life of constant stress, crisis, and urgency can become an addiction. And though it can make for an interesting life, it will never become a life that you author, one of freedom or choice or healing or building. It is a life that never allows you to take the wheel, a life that always remains small.

Change is messy. Change is uncomfortable. Change is strange. But, change is necessary if you're going to reach for your Magic Number and a bigger, better, happier, and more fulfilling life.

So, since this book is essentially a treatise on how to live that magical life, let's get back to how that's done.

Twenty years ago, I came up with the concept of each of us having our own Magic Number. Since then, I've developed and refined this concept, creating a proven method to calculate people's Magic Numbers and build a plan to get there. The methods are uncommon common sense, and they apply to everyone.

A MATTER OF CHOICE NOW, BUT NOT LATER

I've seen firsthand how knowing their Magic Numbers transforms the journeys of many of my clients. People who are toward the end of their working careers or approaching retirement have clarity on how much money they can afford to spend, which takes away the worry and stress. It enables those starting out on their journeys to be clear on what career, business, and financial choices they need to make to reach the point when work is optional. And it empowers people who are partway through their journeys to get absolute clarity on what the next ten years or so need to deliver. Many people, especially those in their 40s and 50s, are realizing that they only have a certain number of working years left and need to make them count.

Because most people don't know their Magic Numbers, and because so many people are not planning for their futures, a large percentage of the population face having to work in their old age because they won't have enough money to support themselves. If you don't have clarity about—and plan for—your future, then the question you have to ask yourself is, "After having worked hard all my life, do I still want to be competing for jobs in my old age?"

Clearly, it's a matter of choice *now*, but it won't be a matter of choice later.

The way to avoid being in a position of having no choice is to take time *now* to establish where you are, where you want to be, and build a plan to get there. To do this, the first thing to know is your Magic Number!

I should alert you, however, that your Magic Number is most likely bigger than you expect. Please don't be put off by this. More people than you know have reached financial independence, even after a slow start. You can too.

With the purchase of this book, I'm delighted to provide you with three months' free access to MagicFuture.com—a website I've created to help you identify your Magic Number and work the MAGIC Formula. Visit StefanWissenbach.com/SDMMbonus and follow the instructions to receive your personal code. Then, in less than ten minutes, you can get started with all the great online tools of the site, including calculating your own unique Magic Number.

Magic Action

Complete Magic Action #7 in your workbook: "What's Your Magic Number?"

Simply choose the type of home(s) you want to enjoy, the vacations you'd like to take, and how you'd like to spend time with those you love. Then, a complex algorithm behind the scenes calculates your Magic Number—the net worth at which work will be optional for you.

The site also helps you understand the gap you need to close in order to reach that point or, if you are very fortunate, confirms you already have. The great thing about knowing this is that it makes your life very straightforward—you have either too much money or not enough. While too much money is the nicer of the two problems, knowing your Magic Number helps you make smart choices about *where* you allocate your money.

If you're like most people and have a gap to close, it's very helpful to know what that gap is and what you need to do to close it. Knowing your Magic Number provides you with a context and decision-making framework to do the right things from this point on.

THE ROAD TO YOUR MAGIC NUMBER

Let me explain how we are going to tackle your number and get you moving into a position where work is optional.

First, please don't be daunted by your number.

Providing you've been truthful, thought about what's important to you, and made choices that truly represent what you desire, your number is accurate and achievable. In some cases, people have Magic Numbers based on a desired lifestyle that's substantially different than where they are today. That's okay—as long as the gap they have to close doesn't become *demotivational.* If this is the case for you, I recommend making choices about your future lifestyle that are less ambitious, but still an acceptable place to be when work is optional, and set out to achieve this first. It's no good killing your motivation before you've started!

Because you are becoming a person with clarity, focus, and direction, every action you take—no matter how small—will bring you closer to achieving the lifestyle you desire. With more action comes more achievement, and with more achievement comes more momentum.

Because you are becoming a person with clarity, focus, and direction, every action you take—no matter how small—will bring you closer to achieving the lifestyle you desire.

Second, it's not just about how much you save; it's about how much you *grow.*

Your personalized profile at MagicFuture.com tells you

the amount you have to *grow* your wealth base each day, month, or year to achieve your Magic Number at the age you want work to be optional. It's important to remember that as you grow your wealth, it will work *for* you, reducing the amount you need to allocate to savings every month to achieve your Magic Number.

For example, if the value of your assets—your home, 401(k), savings, etc.—increased by $20,000 in a year, this is $20,000 put towards your Magic Number. In other words, it's $20,000 less that you have to set aside to stay on target.

It's also important to remember that building your wealth is not just about the money you have. It's also building your personal skills, talents, and knowledge—which leads to the *ability* to generate more wealth.

Third, start small, allow things to grow big, and don't be put off!

Even if you currently can't save or grow your wealth by the amount that you need to be on track to achieve your Magic Number, doing *something* is better than nothing.

If you change nothing, you will make no progress.

In the beginning, the *habit* of saving is more important than the actual *amount* being saved. In his best-selling book, *Start Late, Finish Rich*, David Bach writes about the "latté factor": how the simple act of just saving money on *coffee* each day can make a substantial difference in your wealth over a lifetime. Putting away $3.00 per day, for example, adds up to more than $1,000 in a year. Once the savings habit becomes ingrained, you can set aside more.

The following Magic Action will help you make a list for one week of all the things you spend money on. At the end of the week, review the list and see what of those things you could have done without. Calculate how much you could save each month by eliminating those things. You may be pleasantly surprised.

Magic Action

Complete Magic Action #8 in your workbook: "Disappearing Dollars."

Fourth, when you can, pay down debt.

As you pay down debt, your wealth goes up! Paying interest on other people's money is a real enemy of wealth creation—especially when interest rates are high. One of the quickest ways to start building your wealth base is to start paying down debt, which is costing you money on a monthly basis. Over time, this will dramatically improve your ability to save.

Unless you can make more money with the money you save (i.e. the interest you earn on a savings or investment account is *higher* than the interest being charged on your debt), you should always pay down debt first. Once accomplished, the money you were using to pay down your debt can now be used to increase your savings.

Review your debt and make reducing it a priority. This Magic Action will help with this.

Complete Magic Action #9 in your workbook: "The Debt-Elimination Strategy."

Magic Action

The Magic of Visualization

There have been many studies, books, and audio programs produced on the power of visualization, much more information than I can provide here. My objective, then, is to get you started with a practice that will make a real difference in staying truly connected to your goals and bigger future.

For me, visualization is all about future clarity. It's the power of what I call "wide-awake dreaming," bringing that future into sharp focus with images that energize and excite you. The best way to do this is to create a "vision board," a visual representation of the things you want to achieve.

Interestingly, the first time I created a vision board was in my early teens, and I didn't even realize the power of what I was doing at the time. But I've always been somebody who gets excited and focused about different aspects of life. At that time, I was intensely passionate about BMX bikes. I had pictures on my bedroom wall of BMXers doing tricks, and the pride of place in the middle of my wall was a photo of the bike I dreamed about—a Torker 280x. It was shiny chrome with yellow lettering and had the most fabulous black Skyway five-spoke wheels. There was no way I could afford this bike. I was in school, had no job, and my mother was working shifts to earn enough money to support the family. But I really wanted that bike! I used to go to bed at night dreaming about it; I'd wake up in the morning and there was the photo on my wall. I became so crazy about BMX that I would go to the park to watch the BMXers, who would occasionally let me ride their bikes. Then, my friends started getting their own bikes as the BMX craze really took off. I'd go with them to the BMX park—often having to hitch a ride. That picture stayed on my wall, and the more I got into BMX, the more I wanted that bike.

> If you focus on something enough, the universe has a way of delivering it to you or making it happen.

Then, one day, I was offered the opportunity to go with my friend, Jeff, and his father to the BMX store. I jumped at the chance, as it was a wonderful opportunity to browse and maybe even see this fabulous bike I wanted. Sure enough, there it was in the store—the Torker 280x.

A few days later, Jeff's father arrived at my apartment with the bike. I was speechless. My mother was embarrassed. I was delighted! My friend's father had watched from afar, having picked up his son many times from the BMX park, and seen me there—passionate, happy, but without a bike! He'd seen my reaction and my persistence, and I hadn't once asked anyone to buy me a bike. Realizing we had very little money as a family, he decided to buy the bike for me. It was a very kind gesture and, over 30 years later, I am writing about it and still eternally grateful.

People who deeply subscribe to the power of visualization believe in the law of attraction: that if you focus on something enough, the universe has a way of delivering it to you or making it happen.

I don't think it's so important whether or not you believe in visualization this ardently. Just know that having a vision board is a proven way to keep your goals and aspirations front of mind, and thus helps you to achieve more of what's really important to you.

So why does it work? Well, quite simply, at its most basic level, a vision board keeps you connected to what you are trying to do. If you see it day in and day out, and the images are ones that inspire and motivate you, don't you think it's more likely your daily actions will be aligned with that vision?

Of course they will. It's common sense.

The main reason most people don't achieve great things or fulfill their potential is because they don't consistently follow through, or they allow themselves to get knocked off course. If you're not thinking about your goals, it's easy to get distracted.

A vision board is powerful because, at a glance, you get to see and connect with all the things you want in one collage. It's not laborious, it doesn't take time, and it's emotionally uplifting.

My first vision board was made from cardboard, scissors, and a stick of glue—and displayed images from lots of magazines of things that inspired me! I stuck it on the back of my bedroom door so that I'd see it the first thing every day. It was a great mental jolt.

Paper crafting still works fine, but nowadays smart phones and tablets give you other options to carry your vision board with you. With your three months' free subscription to MagicFuture.com, you can quickly and easily create an online vision board to take with you wherever you go. Update it, download it, print it, set it as a screensaver, or even share it with friends.

Complete Magic Action #10 in your workbook: "Create Your Magic Vision Board."

Magic Action

Most importantly, if you just look at it once a day, it will focus your attention, keep you inspired, and fuel your motivation as you move down the road to your bigger life.

• • • • •

As I've said, you will not get very far on the road to success without motivation. It's only common sense that we'll throw ourselves into endeavors we love far more than those we merely like. However, there are many people who get stuck in a state of motivation, forever excited about their ideas and projects but yet doing very little to bring them to fruition. After all, if you stay at this point, you have all the joy of enthusiasm without the worry of risk! So, it only follows then that the next part of the MAGIC Formula is Application. Think of a steam engine—motivation is your steam; application is your engine. Steam without an engine just blows all over the place or dissipates into the air. So, let's now build an engine to harness your steam and drive you forward toward success.

ROUND-UP

- ❑ I've written down the 10 Magical Things about myself.
- ❑ I've built my motivation foundation by doing the "What's Really Important" exercise.
- ❑ I've determined what "My Question" is.
- ❑ I've gone to MagicFuture.com and discovered my Magic Number.
- ❑ I've reviewed my debt and made reducing it a priority.
- ❑ I've created my Vision Board, either in physical form or using the tools on MagicFuture.com.

A

Application

"You will come to learn, just as I have, Neo,
that there is a difference between
knowing the path and walking the path."
MORPHEUS, *The Matrix*

NOW, IT'S TIME TO EXPLORE THE "A" IN MAGIC, which stands for *application*—taking action, applying yourself to the task at hand, and getting things done. "A" doesn't stand for action because application encompasses both the taking of action and *the way in which you do it.* When you apply yourself, you tend to do so with purpose, intent, and focus—gaining better results than from simply taking action. Action without application is an easy way to deceive yourself that you're making good progress.

So, we're going to transform all the motivation you gained in the first section of this book into a plan—your path to a bigger, brighter, better future. You'll learn how to set goals and get things done. By the end of this section, you'll be more confident, less overwhelmed, and eager to get going.

It's not uncommon for a school report card to read, "Would do so much better if he just applied himself a little bit more." Now, it's been a while since I've looked at mine, but that may very well have been a statement written about me. Was I completing the lessons the teachers were assigning? Of course, but was I *applying* myself? Possibly not. If you use your motivation to apply yourself to the task at hand, you'll achieve far more than just going through the motions. And this is how successful people approach all their serious pursuits, projects, and goals. So, let's look at how *they* apply themselves.

Be Action Oriented

Most significantly, successful people take action—period. They don't dally about, considering this and that or daydreaming about crossing the finish line. They'll deliberate, yes, but only as long as necessary before *moving forward.* And they won't dwell on the possibilities, good or bad, for too long. You may have heard the saying, "Imperfect action is much better than perfect inaction." That's exactly the mantra to keep in mind. In fact, Nike summed it up so succinctly with their brilliant slogan—"Just Do It!"

Of course, it's foolish to rush into things without any thought whatsoever, but after considered thought or analysis the best thing you can do is simply begin. Successful people know "the journey of a thousand miles begins with a single step" and "overanalysis leads to paralysis." The average person, conversely, will dwell in overanalysis, which will mask itself as wise deliberation. This will manifest in countless clever forms—endless surveys of friends and colleagues about a key decision, waiting for approval from someone whose approval isn't actually needed, bottomless digging for information, and more. Long after the success-bound person has set sail on her journey, the typical person is still comfortably sitting on Someday Isle—"Someday, I'll... go after my dreams and goals, just as soon as everything is in place." Well, I'm guessing at this point you've gotten my message: everything will never be in place. Creation is a messy and fluid process, and certainty is never a guarantee, so just take that first step. And then another. And then another.... But of course, action without a plan is like steam without an engine, so let's look at how to build that engine.

From Hoping to Planning

People are funny creatures. Most of us do the same things, day in, day out. Very little changes. Yet, the same people often talk about how their lives will be *different* one day and how things will *change*. Sadly, they probably won't. When you do the same things every day, it's not very likely that your outcomes will ever be different. Why would they? Well, sure, you could get lucky. Some people will take the time every week to buy a lottery ticket, hoping for that big break—but really, the overwhelming odds are, that break will never come. Hope is a great thing to have, but it's no substitute for a plan. If the lottery-ticket-buyers would only spend the same amount of time, energy, and consistency on something that's more likely to make a genuine difference, the chances are far greater that it would bring about a substantial improvement in their lives.

So, beyond being more realistic in how you apply yourself, you need a plan. History shows us that people with plans achieve far more than people without plans. However, the *best* plans are flexible, adaptable, and executed at the appropriate time.

On May 25, 1961, President John F. Kennedy delivered a special message to Congress and, in part, said:

> "I believe that this nation should commit itself to achieving the goal, before this decade is out, of landing a man on the moon and returning him

> safely to the earth. No single space project in this period will be more impressive to mankind, or more important for the long-range exploration of space; and none will be so difficult or expensive to accomplish."

When Kennedy spoke these words, the desired achievement was clearly stated. Did NASA subsequently figure everything out as they went along, going week to week without key milestones and objectives—without a *plan*? Of course not. And with something so new and unprecedented as a trip to the moon, did the plan they start with end up working to the letter, without any changes along the way? Of course not. There were countless adjustments. However many contingencies they'd planned for, there was no way they could foresee them all.

People happily spend hours and hours planning their next vacation while investing little or no time at all planning their *lives*.

And, as a result of an exciting goal and a proper plan—motivation combined with application—the world watched in awe on July 20, 1969 as Neil Armstrong spoke his famous words after setting foot on the moon: "That's one small step for [a] man, one giant leap for mankind."

Though very few people's plans include walking on the moon, it's important to bear in mind the correlation between the likelihood of any goal's success and the preparation that precedes it. And for this reason, I find it curious that most people take time to create a written plan for their deaths—a will—before they've created one for their lives! Don't misunderstand me—wills are important, because they can prevent a lot of problems. But surely a written plan for while you're alive is equally important, not to mention more enjoyable!

On an even more pedestrian level, people will happily spend hours and hours planning their next vacation while investing little or no time at all planning their *lives*. (Some people can't even go a single day on vacation without planning it!) Not only that, they truly enjoy planning the vacation and get excited about what lies ahead. Why not apply this same enthusiasm to all of our living days? Just as a properly planned vacation is a rewarding and fulfilling experience, so is a properly planned life.

Before we continue, an important note—great plans are not rigid. They're flexible; they adapt. When I sit with successful entrepreneurs, I often ask if they had a business plan when they started out. "Of course," they'll say. Then, I'll ask, "If we took that plan out of the drawer and looked at it today, would your business currently resemble that plan to the letter?" This normally draws a smile, because the answer is invariably "no." As the business grew and the people involved learned more, they saw new opportunities, found different and better ways of doing things, and applied their learning to generate greater results.

So, plans need to be flexible and, in the same way businesses and important projects have plans, you need one for your life—to fulfill your potential, be happier, and reach the point when work is optional.

Your Very Own "Treasure Map"

Remember childhood stories about pirates of the high seas? What were they always after? That's right, treasure! And before sailing off to find it, what did they need? A map! While the treasure was the most valuable thing they sought, you could argue that the map was equally valuable since they couldn't find the treasure without it.

But now we've grown up, and the excitement of treasure and treasure maps has been, for many, left in childhood memories or reserved for children's bedtime stories. This is a shame, because there's no reason why the same excitement can't apply to your life right now. We all have our own definition of "treasure," and it may not be material things—it could be getting in better shape, learning an instrument, starting a business, owning a dream home, or buying a car you've always wanted. *You* get to decide what will be *your* treasure and where "X" marks the spot!

The Importance of Writing It Down

How often do you think pirates went out on their voyages seeking treasure without a map? I'm guessing rarely or never. I can't quite see them trusting it all to be in the head of one guy. Likewise, you'll be far more likely to reach your goals with your "map" laid out on paper, or at least the digital equivalent. Putting your plan in writing does a number of things:

• It introduces color and depth into the plan. When you start putting your plan on paper, all sorts of thoughts, details, and aspects come flooding forth that you may not have had when the plan was only in your mind. For example, with a business venture you may start describing your ideal clientele, how your store will be set up, what your logo might look like, and so on. Those things may not contribute materially to the plan's execution, but they will certainly contribute to your involvement and excitement.

"Whatever the mind can conceive and believe, it can achieve."
–Napoleon Hill

• It can highlight flaws or issues. Have you ever started explaining to someone an idea of yours, one that seemed very solid in your mind, and suddenly found yourself at a loss for words? What you thought was a concrete concept was now as loose as gravel. The same happens when you put your plans in written word. The holes, shortcomings, and questionable elements all become more evident—and therefore available to address or solve.

• It can provide additional insight. Seeing your plan in writing, not to mention the actual act of writing it down, may elucidate things about it you wouldn't have otherwise thought of. Your two-week trip to Southeast Asia, plotted out on paper, now has you realizing that Australia is not that far away, you've always wanted to go there, and it's entirely possible to adjust your itinerary to include it.

• And importantly, it captures your plan into physical form and makes it your own. We're living in a very digital world these days, but this recent evolution hasn't erased our desire for the tangible. For example, people still value physical books (you have this one!), making things by hand, and possessing material items. The ones and zeroes of the digital world haven't supplanted the atoms of the real world so far, and I truly don't think they ever will. Being able to physically hold, show, and share your plans gives you a sense of ownership that just isn't the same when it's either only in your head or in a cluster of code on your computer. And I highly recommend investing a bit of time dressing up your plan, however you can, to make it more visually appealing—especially the more important it is. (The Vision Board tool on MagicFuture.com is great for this.) Doing so will heighten your emotional investment and pride.

To continue with that last point, there's a tremendous sense of connection and reinforcement when you commit something to writing, and particularly on paper. I also believe that a written plan dramatically increases your chances for success. And last but not least, as you accomplish each step, you can check it off, which helps you stay motivated and keep your momentum going.

Worry and Course-Correction

Just before I wrote this book, my teenage son and I sat down for a great father-son conversation. He had an exciting couple of years ahead of him as he finished his studies and completed a "gap year" overseas. But he was really worried about what would happen after that—especially when, in these difficult times, young people are finding it increasingly challenging after college. It was clear that his worry and concern were overshadowing his short-term thoughts and actions, not to mention enjoyment.

This happens to all of us from time to time. We allow worry, about what may or may not happen, to creep into our lives and adversely impact our wellbeing in the present. This then affects our short-term performance, which can then hinder or wreck our long-term results. As you see, that can be a dangerous loop. Furthermore, it's been said, over 90% of the things we worry about never come true, and 90% of the things that do come true don't really matter in the long run!

Sadly, some people genuinely have a fear of the future and consequently bury their heads in the sand. My biggest fears, on the other hand, are a life not fulfilled, mediocrity, and an undesirable financial future. The good thing is, these are fears that can be addressed by having a plan. What it comes down to is this—people who have a vision, a plan, passion, and focus don't tend to be scared of the future. They've come to take *ownership* of their lives, instead of worrying about circumstances that are unpredictable or out of their control.

People who have a vision, a plan, passion, and focus don't tend to be scared of the future. They've come to take *ownership* of their lives, instead of worrying about circumstances that are unpredictable or out of their control.

So, how do you create your own treasure map—your plan? Once you have your vision, work it back to the present, and outline the actions you can be taking right now that matter. (This is an excellent use of your Magic Map.) This will help you to live life with purpose. If you *must* worry, concern yourself with what needs to be done today, this week, or this month—not something in the farther and highly unpredictable future. I heard someone once say, "Sometimes, on the way to your dream, you get lost and find a better one." This is so true. The world is fluid and evolving by the minute, and our visions for our futures will change as we progress. Therefore, it is simply best to remain unattached to any expectations, good or bad, about the longer term, because circumstances will undoubtedly change. Conversely, you have far more control over your immediate future, so put your attention there.

My 3-1-90 Approach

It's time now to create your plan.

With the work done earlier in the Motivation chapter—around identifying what's really important to you, determining your question, arriving at your Magic Number, and creating your vision board—you already have everything you need to create your plan. At this point, complete the following Magic Action or visit MagicFuture.com to use the Magic Goals tool.

Magic Action

Complete Magic Action #11 in your workbook: "Your Magic Plan."

Essentially, you will create your plan by capturing all the things you want to *be*, *do*, and *have*, while setting the dates by which you want to achieve them. Some of your goals will be short term; some will be long term. Once you've identified them, you're going to choose your top five. (You'll be able to come back to the others later.)

This is important: I want you to focus on *five or fewer* because, from experience, focusing on too many at once usually leads to achieving very little. Whether you're the type of person who can manage five goals or who needs to focus on just one at a time is personal to you. The only "right" number is the one *you* can successfully manage. The important thing is to be honest with yourself and do what's right for you. If your maximum is three, then doing five will lead to frustration and failure, whereas far more success will arise if you focus on three or fewer. Err on the side of too few than too many; this is especially true at the beginning, when you are most prone to dejection. Ultimately, you will know when you are in control of the situation and ready to introduce another goal.

With your top goals listed, break the journey down by identifying where you need to be in three years, one year, and 90 days for each goal. You'll start by thinking long range because this will make things easier for you. If any of your top goals need to be achieved within less than three years, start by listing that goal and its desired end date and then work back from that point, including your one-year and 90-day timelines.

The great thing about thinking down the road is that you are taken *out* of the complications of the present. When your mind goes to the future, you mentally bypass all the complexity that exists at the moment and are able to think and focus on your vision, free and clear of your current circumstances and issues. This is another valuable lesson I learned from my coach many years ago.

Finally, capture the short-term and immediate actions that need to be taken to get you started—the single first step in the journey of a thousand miles. Once your goal-setting has been completed, be sure to transfer your results to your Magic Map.

Six Success Strategies to Bypass Pervasive Pitfalls

Because I'd like you to be happy and successful, I naturally want to minimize your chances of failure. So, let's spend some time understanding how things *could* go wrong and how to best deal with them. This will allow you to be prepared with some strategies to set you up for success. The following Magic Action will provide you with a way to assess your status with these strategies and capture any insights you may have as you read through them.

Complete Magic Action #12 in your workbook: "Six Success Strategies."

SUCCESS STRATEGY #1: AVOID FEELING OVERWHELMED

At the point you need to turn your motivation into action and application, you may find yourself feeling overwhelmed when you look at your list of goals and actions. But don't worry—be a tugboat.

When a tugboat prepares to pull an ocean liner, it initially fires a weight attached to a small but strong silk string to connect the two vessels. The crew then pulls on the string, which is connected to a rope. Then, they reel in the rope, which is attached to a big chain. Finally, this big chain is used to securely connect the tugboat to the ocean liner. It isn't practical or possible to throw the chain from the tug to the liner, and neither the silk line nor the rope is strong enough to enable the tug to tow the liner, so this process brilliantly solves the problem!

Follow the tugboat's approach: The big heavy chain and the liner represent your goal, the rope your medium-term objectives, and the silk line the things you need to do, often very small, to start making progress right now. The secret to achieving goals is to *think big but start small*, rather than trying the impossible task of "lifting and throwing big chains."

Believe it or not, in most cases, 80% of a task is just getting started.

Believe it or not, in most cases, 80% of a task is just getting started. Often, the best way to get things done is to pick the *smallest* action (the silk line) you can take that will start to build the momentum—then do it! Once you've done one, do the next. For example, let's suppose your goal is to go for a run in the mornings. If you're someone who finds it difficult to get going in the morning, the first small action may be to simply put your sneakers and running gear by your bed before you go to sleep—while you're full of intention. The next small action will be to just get out of bed when the alarm goes off. The third will be to put on the sneakers (and of course, clothes!). The fourth will be to leave the house. I remember having this conversation with a friend of mine who said that, by the time he'd gotten to the point where he was standing outside his front door, awake and in his running gear, it was *easy* to go for a run! Rather than facing what was perceived as one big action, momentum was already there with four small actions taken—just like the silk line, rope, and chain.

SUCCESS STRATEGY #2: AVOID GETTING DISTRACTED OR LOSING FOCUS

If you're new to the principles in this book, it'll be easy for you to get distracted or lose focus and slip back into your old ways. Accept that this is normal. The best thing to do is set yourself up so that you're good at *avoiding* distractions and things that cause you to lose focus. Sounds obvious. But how do you do it?

> Your Magic Hour is a wonderful opportunity to build your motivation, create connection with your bigger future, and set yourself up for a day of accomplishment.

It's all about your "magic hour." For me, this is at the very beginning of each day, when I look at my vision board, Magic Map, goals, actions, and my day and week ahead. This time (whenever it is for you) is a wonderful opportunity to build your motivation, create connection with your bigger future, and set yourself up for a day of accomplishment. It's tremendously helpful in preparing to deal with obstacles that arise and, importantly, as we covered earlier regarding your vision, be attuned to opportunities that are in harmony with where you are trying to go. If you have a bad day, and we all do from time to time, use the next day's magic hour as an opportunity to get back on track, instead of letting one bad day turn into two or more. For more about the magic hour concept, see page 69 in the Independence section.

SUCCESS STRATEGY #3: AVOID TRYING TO DO TOO MUCH

Attempting to tackle too many things is quite common—especially if you've done a great job of throwing yourself into the "M" in MAGIC and building your motivation. It's very easy with lots of motivation and excitement for a bigger future, especially if you toss in a dash of confidence, to end up with a big to-do list. Big lists themselves aren't the problem—the problem is when people try to do too many things on the list at the same time. Think of accomplishment as catching rabbits. Chase them all at once, and the chances are you'll catch none. Single them out one at a time, focus on one at a time, and you'll catch them one at a time. Before you know it, you'll have ten. In the meantime, the person who chased all ten probably still has none.

Steve Jobs, the co-founder of Apple who died in 2011, left a legacy as a wonderful man who impacted the lives of literally millions and has been heralded as the most successful CEO of the past 25 years. Clearly an extremely talented individual, he differentiated himself from everyone else by believing that it's not the things you do, but the things you *don't do*, that make the biggest difference in your success.

I think this is a unique and insightful way to look at life. Many people have plans and daily objectives—but once you've defined these objectives, being successful is about having the discipline *not* to do things that will distract you from, or sabotage, your goals.

SUCCESS STRATEGY #4: STAYING ON COURSE

Getting off track is as normal for people as breathing. We're an easily distracted bunch! It's a way of life, and the best thing you can do is not waste emotional energy by getting upset over it—instead, just embrace it as being human. And the good thing is, we humans can be quite resilient. We can experience horrific disasters, things outside our control, and still bounce back to inspire those around us. My friend Mike Wilson (who founded a billion-dollar business from scratch) said to me over 15 years ago, "Good people are like quality shares (stocks) in a business. Things happen that cause them to be down from time to time. But whether they're down is not important; it's expected to happen. What matters is how quickly they bounce back."

It's wise advice, and I want you to remember it. You will get knocked down; it's normal. So when you do, brush yourself off and bounce back. Likewise, when you get off course, don't dwell on it or beat yourself up about it—just get back on your way toward your goals.

SUCCESS STRATEGY #5: ORGANIZE YOUR LIFE AROUND YOUR GOALS RATHER THAN YOUR GOALS AROUND YOUR LIFE

The great thing about my MAGIC Formula for happiness and success is that you end up with goals and visions that are naturally aligned with how you want to live your life.

Organizing your life around your goals is therefore something that brings fulfillment and happiness. Most people, however, end up being passengers rather than pilots, allowing other people, situations, or circumstances to decide the direction of their travel. They end up becoming part of other people's plans. As the great Jim Rohn once said, "If you don't design your own life plan, chances are you'll fall into someone else's plan. And guess what they have planned for you? Not much."

So, it's only natural that frustration will set in if you allow life (and other people in it) to dictate your goals, either directly or by default. Better to be proactive and take control of what you want out of life. For example, don't let the crowd you hang around with determine your aspirations—let your aspirations determine the crowd you hang around with. In doing so, you'll often avoid wasting time on things (and people!) that aren't important and accomplish more of the things you want to do.

"If you don't design your own life plan, chances are you'll fall into someone else's plan. And guess what they have planned for you? Not much."
–Jim Rohn

We have a great exercise we use my office to teach the value of doing what's important first. It works particularly well with new recruits.

We hand them a container, which has in it three or four rocks, lots of pebbles, and some sand—all held nicely under a tight-fitting lid. We hand them a sieve and a bowl and ask them to empty the container, sieving the sand into the bowl first and then separating the rocks from the pebbles.

We then ask them to put everything back into the container, starting with the sand, followed by the pebbles, and then the rocks. We ask them to put the lid on. Guess what? It doesn't fit. It won't fit, no matter how they try. We then explain to them that the container represents a working day (and by extension, your life). The sand represents minutia and small unimportant tasks; the pebbles represent slightly more important actions; and the rocks represent the truly important things that need to get done. We then ask them to empty the container again and try putting everything back, thinking about their perfect day and what they would do first. Clearly, the first thing they put in are the rocks. They follow with the pebbles, which fall down the big gaps between the rocks. Finally, the sand goes in and works its way into all the little nooks and crannies (sometimes with the help of a little shake). And like magic, the lid fits on the container!

It's a very simple but brilliant exercise we should all keep in mind throughout our day-to-day lives. Get the big rocks in first, because it seldom matters if we finish our day with sand left to do.

SUCCESS STRATEGY #6: GETTING HELP AND ACCOUNTABILITY

We all need the help and support of others. In fact, the most brilliant people are those who realize their brilliance is *because of* their community—not in spite of it. (This is so important that I devote the final chapter of this book to it.) Accept that you can't do it all by yourself, and if you're struggling and feel you would benefit from someone else's input, *ask for it!* It's a sign of strength, not weakness. And yet so many people plow ahead stubbornly—when asking for a bit of help, guidance, or support could accelerate their progress immensely.

Unless you posses superhuman powers of discipline and focus, you'll benefit from a little accountability. Not being accountable to ourselves or others makes it very easy for us to slip, push things back, not get things done, or take the path of least resistance—rather than the path less travelled. One of the great benefits I get from flying across the Atlantic every 90 days to meet my coach and fellow entrepreneurs is that every time I get on that airplane, I want to have my stuff done. I want to have completed my 90-day objectives. I'm in an environment with success-oriented, highly accomplished people, and I don't want to be there feeling like I didn't follow through!

Accountability is very powerful, so I encourage you to either create a magic team—I'll explain how I do this in the Community section—or find other ways of making yourself accountable. For instance, simply let another person know that you'll have something done by a certain date—then you'll look bad if you don't. Another method is to not allow yourself to do or get something you really want until you've accomplished an important task. Lastly, remember to use our goal-sharing tool at MagicFuture.com as a great way to set up accountability for yourself.

* * * * *

I hope by now you've fully grasped why this chapter is entitled *Application* instead of *Action*—there is so much more to be accomplished through sincerely applying yourself as opposed to just doing, doing, doing. But at the root of it is developing an action mindset and being oriented toward setting and reaching goals. This is what transforms hopes and dreams into written plans and reality. We are very habitual creatures, so use this to your advantage in maintaining "habitual progress"; once you are in the rhythm of taking constant steps toward your goals, you'll find it easier to keep up—and indeed strange and uncomfortable when progress isn't being made!

By the same token, however, don't fall into the trap of becoming so driven that you're thrown off when things don't go as you'd expected. Better yet, shed expectations, remaining instead focused on—but not *attached to*—your goals. This will help you buffer yourself against the inevitable rough patches, alleviate much worry, and make it easier to incorporate the success strategies I outlined in the past several pages.

Perhaps the greatest thing that comes from applying

yourself, however, is not the accomplishments that result, but rather the personal growth you acquire in the process. Ultimately, our ability to learn from our adventures and transform ourselves for the better is what makes the difference in the quality of our lives. So, after you've checked off the Round-Up on the next page, let's explore growth and its part in the MAGIC Formula.

ROUND-UP

- ❑ I've created my Action Plan for my 90-day, one-year, and three-year goals either using the exercise in the back of this book or the Magic Goals tool at MagicFuture.com.
- ❑ I understand and commit to Success Strategy #1 to avoid feeling overwhelmed in my goals.
- ❑ I understand and commit to Success Strategy #2 to avoid getting distracted or losing focus.
- ❑ I understand and commit to Success Strategy #3 to avoid trying to do too much at once.
- ❑ I understand and commit to Success Strategy #4 to stay on course.
- ❑ I understand and commit to Success Strategy #5 to get help from others as I pursue my goals.
- ❑ I understand and commit to Success Strategy #6 to organize my life around my goals, instead of organizing my goals around my life.
- ❑ I understand and commit to Success Strategy #7 to get accountable with a Goal Buddy or Magic Team.

G

Growth

> "We cannot solve our problems with the same thinking we used when we created them."
>
> ALBERT EINSTEIN

I THINK EACH AND EVERY ONE OF US owes it to ourselves to be the best we can be. Not in comparison to others, but truly being the best *we* can be—and that means growing into the person we want to become.

None of us arrives on the planet knowing what to do or how, exactly, to do it. We learn over time and with experience and instruction. The mistake we make is thinking that, having reached a certain age, our growing is over. And *that* could not be further from the truth. In many ways, after childhood has ended, learning the true ropes of human life has just begun.

The key to taking control in every aspect of your life, the key to achieving more and loving the journey—including reaching your Magic Number—is understanding that learning and growth are lifelong companions. And if you want to travel down the path to success, you need to rigorously transfer that learning into meaningful action and apply that action to create change.

There is breadth and depth to the subject of growth, but before I tackle that topic, I'd like to discuss some personal attributes I feel are necessary to lay the groundwork for meaningful change. These qualities are (a) cultivating self-awareness and (b) being coachable. They are the fertile soil that will nourish your growth, and subsequent success, in every area of your life.

Self-Awareness

What is self-awareness? For the most part, it's simply being alert and aware of how your communication, behaviors, actions, and appearance impact other people.

I find it astonishing that so many people lack self-awareness.

Our environments condition us—all of us—and we are victim to our habits and ways of doing things. But once you're at a stage of life where you know your own mind, you can decide who you are and who you'd like to be. It's not up to anyone else. You have to make that conscious decision. Quite often, most of us carry on doing what we've always done, without giving any real thought to what that truly means. Happiness and fulfillment, however, require a keen sense of self-awareness. The truly successful are aware of the way they talk, the tone of voice they use, the way they dress, the things they say, and the impact this will have on other people. If you can become more self-aware and understand the consequences of your behaviors and actions, you will have the power to decide whether to change them or not. If you don't understand the impact you have, you are powerless to change. We all have the capability to decide how to present ourselves to the world.

As the saying goes, you only get one chance to make a first impression. As you go through life, you will see very quickly how powerful the concept of being self-aware is and appreciate the way you affect others.

Being self-aware is to be cognizant of what you project and how others might see you. This is not to encourage you to be overly concerned with appearances, but just to consider the following: When people look at you, what do you want them to be thinking? If you walked into a room full of people, what would they think before you even said a word? When you speak, what would they think? Do you look them in the eye? Do they listen to you? Do *you* listen to *them*? Self-awareness is a genuine skill because it requires being completely truthful with yourself.

Listening is key. You have two ears and one mouth—use them in proportion. Be *interested*, not interesting. We all know people who are so busy *trying* to be interesting to others—by talking at them too much—that their self-absorption and self-containment turns almost everyone off. And that can include a valuable connection in a person right next to them.

Complete Magic Action #13 in your workbook: "Growth Through Listening."

I once met with a group of lawyers, the most senior of which completely lacked self-awareness. He spent most of our meeting talking about himself and telling jokes that were just not funny. If he'd taken just one second to become more self-aware and tune into the dynamic of the room, it would have been a much more productive meeting—for both of us!

Most people are familiar with Intelligence Quotient, IQ, which is a longtime, though disputed, standard measurement of intellectual capability. A person with an IQ of 100 is considered to have an average intellect; IQs greater or less than 100 indicate an intellect that is greater or less than average. Fewer people, however, are familiar with Emotional Quotient, EQ. A person's EQ is said to reflect her emotional intelligence—or the ability to identify and appraise one's own emotions and the emotions of others—a key component to becoming self-aware. It's not uncommon for a person to have a high IQ but a dismally low EQ. And, I think, EQ is the more important of the two. For instance, the lawyer I mentioned above had exemplary qualifications, but did he pull off the deal? No. He did not. Had he been more self-aware, with a more developed EQ, we would probably be doing business since his firm's capabilities were optimal—but his bulldozing personality and self-absorption had me looking elsewhere for legal advice. One of the simplest ways you can improve your self-awareness is by noticing the quality in others. Next time you go into a shop, for example, reflect afterwards on the service you had and how it made you feel. Take note of what worked and what didn't. Ask yourself how you would've done it differently if *you* were the person driving that customer experience.

With good service, you'll see what's happening: They're making eye contact, listening, and smiling at you; they have open body language and are receptive and eager to help; and most importantly, they're interested in you and the interaction. You can learn a lot from these people about how to attract and leave others with a positive impression.

Magic Action

Complete Magic Action #14 in your workbook: "Growth Through Learning from a Great Service Experience."

Being Coachable

In addition to being observant and aware, true growth requires being receptive to other people's wisdom, feedback, and advice—in other words, being coachable.

You will become a better person when you develop the mindset that feedback is not criticism but rather fuel for your personal growth.

Think of a coachable moment as being the gift of greater knowledge. Most everyone knows the saying "Knowledge is power," but that phrase needs to be amended because—

in truth—knowledge is only power *when applied.* You're not necessarily going to agree with all the knowledge and feedback that comes your way. And sometimes someone you think wouldn't be qualified to provide a "coachable moment" hits you between the eyes with their insight. If you feel the person is giving the appraisal with good intent, embrace it. When someone is giving you a coachable moment, it can be uncomfortable for both of you. Asking you to modify or stop your behavior, or relaying that something you've done has caused a problem can be awkward and confrontational. Remember that, in most cases, the person wouldn't be giving you the feedback if he or she didn't care. Whether you choose to act upon it or not is always entirely up to you. Deep down you'll know whether or not what they said was valuable.

Sometimes someone you think wouldn't be qualified to provide a "coachable moment" hits you between the eyes with their insight.

Conversely, beware of over-complimentary people. It's great to receive a thumbs-up on your actions, but praise, though sometimes well earned, can result in complacency when relied on too heavily—and this kills potential and slows you down. Accept compliments graciously but beware of sycophants, and never confuse flattery for praise. All can be pitfalls lulling you into laziness.

Often, people don't deliver coachable moments because they don't believe you will be receptive to them. The following Magic Action will help you with this. I recommend identifying three people with whom you have regular interaction and whose opinions you respect. Explain to them the concept of a coachable moment and that, because you respect their opinions, you'd like to receive feedback from them on an ongoing basis. If that feedback is not forthcoming periodically—having given them permission to do so—prompt them for it. It's a great way to stay on course.

Complete Magic Action #15 in your workbook: "Being Coachable."

Plan Forwards, Measure Backwards

Now that the fertile ground of cultivating self-awareness and remaining coachable has been laid, it's time to look at the nuts and bolts of fostering growth and evaluating your progress.

A good friend of mine once told me, "What gets measured gets done." As your bigger future unfolds, it's important not only to map out your desired future but to measure and evaluate the path you've just travelled. In other words, look at where you've come from and draw energy, enthusiasm, encouragement, and confidence from everything you've completed. If you aren't where you planned to be, focus on understanding why and applying the lesson; don't get hung up in failure. The greatest teachers in personal development advise you to plan forwards and measure backwards, and that's exactly what we're going to do.

Growth Opportunities

Little did I know when I first started buying personal-development programs over 25 years ago that the information I was absorbing was slowly building a foundation for me to create a great future, narrate my own audio program, write books, and launch a website that enables millions of people all over the world to take control, achieve more, and love life. That's why I encourage you to soak up all the learning possible; you don't always know at the moment how valuable it will become.

There are two types of learning we'll discuss in this chapter:

Day-to-day learning—how you grow from your experiences on a daily, weekly, monthly, and yearly basis

Structured, proactive learning—information you seek out deliberately to obtain a new skill or expertise

We'll begin by evaluating day-to-day experiences. Done consciously, this can be an extremely effective method of identifying your strengths and uncovering where more progress is needed.Not long ago, while telling me about her week at school, my daughter told me her class had voted her Form Captain. She said that she'd declined the position, however, because it would've required a slight amount of additional work. So, I used this moment to teach her how to evaluate opportunities using a pros-and-cons list. Together, we drew a line down the middle of a piece of paper and listed the advantages of the position on one side of the page and disadvantages on the other. By the end of the exercise, and without my having to say anything, it became clear to her that accepting the position would have been the better choice. She has used a pros-and-cons list several times since—a life skill that will serve her well in the future.

The Experience Transformer is a technique that can be used to gain perspective on the outcomes of choices you make and a method I hope will become foundational to your day-to-day learning.

Am I pleased that she declined the position? No. But am I gratified that she learned the lesson and has adopted a new tactic that will help her evaluate decisions in the future? You bet I am. A pros-and-cons list is an integral part of evaluating an opportunity. But because hindsight is 20/20, it's an absolute shame that many people don't deliberately examine an experience *after* it's happened. Consciously reviewing, on paper, how an experience went after the fact can offer invaluable insights and perspective that you'd never have gained otherwise.

This is why my coach, Dan Sullivan, taught me the "Experience Transformer"™* many years ago; it's a technique that can be used to gain perspective on the outcomes of choices you make and a method I hope will become foundational to your day-to-day learning.

The following Magic Action will provide you an interactive way to do an Experience Transformer, but here's the basic process:

* Used here with kind permission of Strategic Coach (StrategicCoach.com).

1. List everything about the experience that worked. Continue to do this until you run out of things to write down. (Resist the temptation, in this step, to think of what *didn't* work.)
2. Now list everything that *did not* work.
3. Write down everything you would do differently, knowing what you know now.
4. Next to each thing you'd do differently, write down how you can transfer that learning into action to generate a more satisfying experience in the future.

Magic Action

Complete Magic Action #16 in your workbook: "Growth Through Learning from an Experience."

This process is so powerful that every Friday on my working weeks, my assistant, Jayne, and I have time dedicated to complete an Experience Transformer for the week just ended. Jayne makes a point of capturing—during the week—things that worked and things that didn't work. (This is also important, because it's easy to forget by Friday what did and didn't work earlier in the week.) The process is also a wonderful way to close off the week, using the exercise to appreciate the learning and progress we've made. It enables us to consistently make incremental improvements, and when I look back to where we were just a few short years ago, I see how much better we are doing things today—all because of how we embrace the Experience Transformer.

Regular Reviews and Maintaining Perspective

Jayne and I complete an Experience Transformer on a weekly basis, but it's equally critical to evaluate your progress over longer timeframes, such as quarterly and annually. I can't emphasize enough the importance of picking a point in the future, deciding where you want to be at that point, and working back to determine what needs to happen *right now* to be on track. Quarterly reviews should include examining the past 90 days' experiences, looking forward to the future, and deciding what you must do next. It's also an ideal opportunity to do a quarterly "anti-virus check"—to maintain your awareness and not slip back into your old ways. Just as a computer virus will slow down your computer, not checking your progress and learning from it will do the same to you. Finally, quarterly growth reviews provide the opportunity to carefully consider the relationships you have that are in harmony with your goals and those that are not—and a chance to do something about it.

Assessing your progress each year offers an even broader context from which to view the road you've just travelled. And, as with all things, it's important to maintain a healthy perspective when looking back.

Let's imagine your life a year from now. Think about the goals you've set and where you've said you'll be at that point. Imagine now that we're a year forward, and you've achieved much of what you set out to achieve. (For this example, let's assume that you haven't yet achieved your Magic Number—but you've made some great progress towards closing the gap.) You could approach your progress over the year in one of two ways: negatively or positively.

Quarterly growth reviews provide the opportunity to carefully consider the relationships you have that are in harmony with your goals and those that are not—and a chance to do something about it.

With a negative perspective, you could look at the reality that you still have a gap between where you are and your Magic Number; you could feel a bit depressed that there's still a long way to go; you could dwell on how much you still have to achieve in many areas of your life; and like most people, you could start feeling so overwhelmed that you find yourself losing motivation.

An alternative—positive—approach, however, would be to look back over the past 12 months and appreciate all the great things you've achieved, recognize all the progress you've made, and marvel at all the new experiences and lessons that have made you a better person over the year. You could also be proud that you've made progress towards your Magic Number, no matter the amount, and are closer to the point where work will be optional. And you could view all of that achievement, learning, and growth as further motivation, to set you up for the next quarter and year of building a better life.

As you see, you can have a negative or positive perspective on precisely the same experience. As with most things in life, you have a choice.

> "Finish every day and be done with it. You have done what you could; some blunders and absurdities crept in—forget them as soon as you can. Tomorrow is a new day. You shall begin it well and serenely, and with too high a spirit to be encumbered with your old mistakes and nonsense."
>
> Ralph Waldo Emerson

Proactive Learning

Regular review of your daily, weekly, quarterly, and yearly experiences is an integral part of your growth process and should always be a part of your strategy to live a bigger, happier, more fulfilled life. But there is another tactic that should be employed as you head down the road to your Magic Number and beyond—the structured study of information and the deliberate, proactive learning of a subject, skill, qualification, or craft.

We have all experienced the growth that comes from structured learning, having been to school and studied various topics. But while you have limited choice on the subjects you study in school, those you study afterward are pretty much up to you.

There's a grave misperception in our culture that structured learning and study stop after we complete our formal education. There could not be a more destructive or damaging notion. In our youth, many of us were led through school by the nose, studying this subject or that, conforming to social pressures, family expectations, or societal conventions. Worse, some of us were never even asked what we wanted to do with our lives or—as bad—expected to know the answer when it came time to declare our college majors, typically only two years after high school. It is an idea that has thwarted promising futures and damaged the most hopeful plans.

Our problem today is not a shortage of information—it is in discerning the useful, accurate, and relevant information from the useless drone of subjective noise.

As time passes, the world changes, and what seemed to be written in granite 25 years ago may not even exist anymore. The skills and training you obtained then may well be obsolete now, and there's a likelihood that your job has gone the way of the horse and buggy or perhaps been outsourced overseas. So, if conventional wisdom says your growth and learning ends with your formal education, it may have sent you way up a creek without a paddle later in life.

Since we can't go back, decide what it is that turns you on, floats your boat, and makes your heart sing *now*. It requires self-awareness, staying open and coachable, and a hefty dose of faith—but it is the first step to a more magical, happy, fulfilled life, and one well worth taking.

And these days, there's no excuse not to learn. An African villager with a smartphone now has access to more information than the president of the United States did 20 years ago. Think about it. Our problem today is not a shortage of information—there's a torrent of worthless, inaccurate, and subjective information barraging us each day. Our problem is in discerning the useful, accurate, and relevant information from the useless drone of subjective noise. And, then, gathering the courage to act upon it.

This starts with making a choice on what it is you want to learn. And this is where it can get really fun—especially when you're following my MAGIC Formula and have clarity on your desired future, vision, and goals.

In my case, ever since I was a young boy, I've been fascinated by helicopters. In fact, I'm still a bit of a helicopter geek. Even now, when a helicopter flies overhead, my kids just roll their eyes and ask, "Okay, Dad, what is it?" They know I'll tell them the make and model. When I felt this drive, I didn't just sit on the passion—I took action. In my late 20s, I obtained my helicopter pilot's license. Now, this learning wasn't related to my business or reaching my Magic Number, but it was hugely rewarding, challenging, and exciting. It has made my life far more interesting and rich ever since.

Though your goal may not be to learn to fly rotary-wing aircraft, there are so many other subjects that will enrich your life, work and personal fulfillment, and are well worth knowing.

Structured learning doesn't always have to take the form of formal classes or large texts. You'll find training in your professional arena, or others, in all sorts of areas you may not have previously thought to look. Here are some options.

> Structured learning is an integral ingredient in the formula for a more magical, fulfilled life.

iTunes U—Download the Apple iTunes software, and you'll have access to iTunes U. Short for iTunes University, this site offers lectures, discussions, and classes on all manner of subjects, from business to engineering, arts to corporate finance, and medicine to politics—all from top universities, museums, and cultural institutions around the world. And it's all for free.

Online Tutorials—Not just for watching cats climb curtains or babies being cooed, the ubiquitous YouTube can also teach you something quickly—from making shortbread cookies to cracking pecans to caulking your bathtub, there's a short instructional video for almost any topic on the website. More formal tutorials are offered by training sites such as Lynda.com or TeamTreehouse.com, which offer a plethora of expert instructional videos on graphic design, web programming, business practices, and software applications, all for a low monthly fee.

Public libraries have been the backbone of learning and growth for millennia, and now they're not just about books anymore. Check out their catalogs online for the many audio and video resources available to borrow. In fact, many libraries offer downloads of digital resources directly to your computer or handheld device for a specific period of time. Listen to audio books on the go and become versed in a new skill or craft from the convenience of wherever you are.

Amazon.com has millions of books and informational materials available, many of them previously owned and priced under $10. Similarly, eBay and Craigslist are websites where people resell, among other things, books and training materials they've already enjoyed, for a fraction of the retail cost.

So, there you have it. No excuse not to learn. A plethora of opportunity abounds. Your only challenge is to take it.

Think about what you love and whether there's a skill, qualification, or craft that you could obtain by focusing some time, energy, and attention to it. Structured learning is an integral ingredient in the formula for a more magical, fulfilled life.

Complete Magic Action #17 in your workbook: "Skills and Knowledge."

Magic Action

Unique Ability

Cultivating self-awareness, staying coachable, conducting weekly, quarterly, and annual reviews, and concentrating on proactive structured learning will, if the stars align and the gods are smiling, ultimately comes down to one thing: discovering your unique ability.

There is so much to pursue and explore in the world for fun, but work that allows you to one day reach your Magic Number is work that requires mastery. And work that requires mastery means narrowing down the topics you'll focus on during your growth. Ultimately, it means zeroing in on a handful of areas that inspire you and, consequently, in which you will most likely excel.

As a result of being coached and staying coachable, the single biggest breakthrough I've experienced in my personal development is the importance of understanding and developing my unique ability. Each and every one of us has skill set that is specific to us, which includes one or two things we're exceptional at doing, a large number of things we're mediocre at doing, and an even larger number of things that we're quite bad at doing. When we're engaged in things that don't match our unique ability, it often feels like tedium and drudgery—*and it drains us*. As a result, we don't perform at our best, we make more mistakes, and we don't fulfill our potential—not a formula for a magical life. On the other hand, when you're operating in your "unique ability zone," work often doesn't feel like work; it feels timeless, fluid, and energizing. Winston Churchill said, "Find a job you love and you'll never work again." That job you love will most likely align with your unique ability.

When you're operating in your "unique ability zone," work often doesn't feel like work; it feels timeless, fluid, and energizing.

I was at a wedding one time where a charming young man seated at my table asked me for advice on how to make his fortune. I explained that he first needed to understand his unique ability. Because he was looking for me to *tell* him what job or business to go into, he was surprised by my answer. Like so many people, he was defining and quantifying success entirely by money alone. As this book is, in large part, a call to build your financial net worth to the point were work is optional—your Magic Number—I understand well the importance money plays in this gritty, grueling, very physical human life. There's not much point in musing over the finer points of your unique ability when you're struggling to keep the lights on and put food on the table. Before that's accomplished, not much else matters.

However, it is my goal in this book to illustrate both the importance of valuing money for what *it* can do and uncovering the more intangible aspects of life that lead to happiness and fulfillment—intellectually, emotionally, even spiritually. It makes little sense to think of one to the exclusion of the others.

And for those who have been raised in religious traditions, it takes only one quick look at the world to see that it is not only the benevolent and noble who forsake all worldly goods. Likewise, it is not only the rich and wealthy that, if justice prevailed, would be banished from the kingdom of heaven. A simple glance at the history of our civilization will easily reveal that.

For me, true success is much more than money; however, money is an imperative component of it.

And those who discount money as lowly or base or unworthy of their consideration do so at their own peril.

That is why I told that young man at the wedding to understand his unique ability, and why I am telling you to do so as well. Enjoying your work leads to more motivation, more engagement, more learning, and thus more mastery—and happily, as a consequence, oftentimes *more* money will follow.

Enjoying your work leads to more motivation, more engagement, more learning, and thus more mastery.

Happy and fulfilled people *find a way to apply what they are highly talented in, as often as possible in their everyday lives, careers, and businesses*.

Frank Sinatra didn't move pianos, sell tickets, or work lights at his shows—he organized things so people around him took care of those tasks, and he could focus only on his performance. When listening to him croon out one of his old standards, I don't think anyone could fault him for that.

This type of zeroing in on your talents is incredibly liberating. My assistant, Jayne, is absolutely brilliant at keeping me focused on my unique ability. Sometimes she has a big job on her hands, but she helps organize my time so I can focus on my specific expertise while delegating things I'm mediocre or terrible at to others. (But please don't try to recruit my Jayne, because she's deliriously happy doing what she does!)

To discover your unique ability or refine your appreciation and understanding of it, ask a number of people who know you for feedback on what they believe your skills, attributes, and qualities are. Of course, their responses are only secondary to the promptings of your own inner voice, but they can nonetheless be illuminating. In the following Magic Action, we've provided a framework to collate and analyze the feedback you receive, find common themes, and ultimately write a statement that captures the essence of who you are.

Magic Action

Complete Magic Action #18 in your workbook: "Your Unique Ability."

Celebrating Your Milestones

"The more you praise and celebrate your life,
the more there is in life to celebrate."
OPRAH WINFREY

We've talked a lot about goal setting and goal reaching, but life, as we've discussed, is not entirely about accumulating accolades and achievements. In fact, none of it is much worth anything unless you celebrate it all along the way.

The road of life always gives you another mountain to move, another dragon to slay. I'm here to implore you *not* to put off celebrating until all the monsters are vanquished and the peaks conquered. Sprinkle revelry throughout the path along your Magic Map. That way, you will be much more likely to enjoy the long and winding journey down it—and *that*, as many of you know, is what life is really all about.

I, myself, am a bit of a celebration fanatic. I love celebrating and having reasons to celebrate. I agree with

Oprah when she says the *more* you celebrate life, the more life *gives* you to celebrate. Be sure to set celebratory tags and markers along your path to your goals, so that as you achieve each milestone, you know what treat and reward lies in store for you. It applies to all goals—personal and work related. And be sure the celebration befits the task. Successfully complete a big deal or achieve a big goal? Big celebration! Complete a smaller task that was somewhat challenging? Smaller celebration!

How you celebrate is entirely up to you. It doesn't have to be elaborate. Mine can be as simple as a toast at mealtime when I'm talking with the family. Or perhaps it's a celebratory meal with some nice wine when acknowledging a bigger achievement. Beyond that, it may be dining out in a great restaurant or staying in an exceptional hotel. Taking some time to do something you truly enjoy is also a great motivator, and it can start you off in a positive mindset when it comes time for the next leg of your journey. Whatever you choose, find a way of celebrating that excites you and, when you achieve a major goal or milestone, let the proverbial champagne corks fly. It's the entire reason we're doing all this in the first place.

Use the following Magic Action to review your goals and forthcoming actions and attach celebratory tags to the ones you think will be the most challenging and worthy of celebrating. Then, celebrate them!

Magic Action

Complete Magic Action #19 in your workbook: "Celebrate!"

* * * * *

Just as a children must experience personal growth in order to achieve independence as adults, we all must master the aspects of personal growth in this chapter before we can work on developing independence in our lives. After you complete the checklist on the following page, we'll dive into how to develop the independent *mindset* that's necessary to truly enjoy an independent lifestyle.

ROUND-UP

- ❑ I am committed to wanting to learn.
- ❑ I understand how to transfer learning to action.
- ❑ I know that I need to apply action through planning forward and then measuring back.
- ❑ I will seek out and be more aware of the two main growth opportunities in my life—day-to-day learning and ongoing study.
- ❑ For day-to-day learning, I will incorporate the Experience Transformer; weekly, monthly, and annual reviews; and celebrate my accomplishments.
- ❑ For ongoing study, I will dedicate myself to becoming more self-aware, becoming more coachable, and determining and appreciating my unique ability.

Independence

> "The greatest thing in the world is
> to know how to belong to oneself."
>
> Ð Michel de Montaigne, *The Complete Essays*

IF THE OBJECTIVE BEHIND MY MAGIC FORMULA could be summed up in one word, it would be the title of this chapter. Without independence, uncovering your motivation, embarking on application, pursuing growth, and even, in some cases, building your preferred community are, essentially, futile efforts. Of course, in the strictest terms, life is about *interdependence*, not independence, because no man is an island, and all our pursuits would be difficult and depressing if we embarked on them totally alone.

However, for the purposes of this book, we are going to talk about independence in the same sense we discussed it in the opening chapters: the ability to spend your time how you wish to spend it, doing the things you love and enjoy, and being in a position where you are mostly not reliant on others.

Of course, a state of dependency can occur any number of ways: physically, politically, socially, psychologically, and emotionally. But even if you're struggling for the baseline of independence—trying to escape a totalitarian regime, looking to get quality healthcare, or move to a safer place to live—a level of *financial* control, even in moderate degrees, can aid you in all those objectives.

A happy, fulfilled life is not about outdoing your neighbors or scrambling for the latest designer-brand this or that. Of course, those things can be fun and part of your road to a more fulfilling life—but as I described earlier, knowing I had the ability to buy a Ferrari by 30 and a Rolls-Royce by 40, and what it took to get to that point, brought more satisfaction than the day the cars were delivered. To whatever extent those things bring a kick of gratification or satisfaction, it is a temporary sensation—it's not a bedrock on which to build your life.

Happiness and fulfillment, dare I say magic, comes from driving your life and its every facet in the direction you choose, in the figurative vehicle you choose to drive it, and with the people you choose to drive with.

It takes courage, brashness, and staking your old comfortable life on a new idea that hasn't even taken form. But it's there for you, and I'll tell you how to move closer towards it in this chapter. The way to achieve and maintain independence is through honing your habits, appreciating your values, monitoring your attitude, and practicing gratitude.

Magic Attitude

Of anything that I think will clear your path to the independence we've discussed, of anything that I believe will move you towards the life you most desire, your attitude will make the most difference.

I used to read my son bedtime stories about valiant

heroes who struck out on epic journeys in search of hidden treasure. On their quests, they faced innumerable obstacles, fiery dragons, and immovable mountains that endangered their journeys and blocked their paths.

After each setback, however, after every lost battle, every fallen comrade, or frontline retreat, the main characters pulled themselves together, gathered up their courage, and pressed onwards, believing that their mission was worthy and achievable.

An exercise in perseverance and persistence, this was also an act of faith—a belief that things *would* get better, the next dragon slain, the next mountain moved; it was a commitment to optimism, a bright perspective and a positive attitude.

An optimistic outlook and positive attitude is one of the most invaluable traits you can possess on your journey. I understand that it doesn't always feel like it, but no matter how dire our circumstances, we always have a choice when it comes to our perspective on the matter.

> No matter how dire our circumstances, we always have a choice when it comes to our perspective.

My dear friend Alex Whitelaw had turned 50 and was enjoying life with his wonderful wife and twin sons when he was diagnosed with terminal cancer; the diagnosis came as a complete shock. No one deserves cancer, of course, and Al was one of the kindest, most generous, fun-loving people I'd ever met. It just seemed so very unfair. I'd known him for over 30 years. If you had met him, the first thing you would've noticed was his fabulous smile and how he always saw the good in everyone; then, he got this devastating news. He had to make a choice about how he approached the rest of his life.

Given the tragedy of the situation, anyone would have totally understood if Alex became dark and negative. After all, the situation really sucked. However, Al came to terms with the diagnosis, decided to adopt a fighter's attitude, and embraced and enjoyed every day.

Despite being told by medical experts he only had 12

months to live, Alex was still enjoying meals with friends in wonderful restaurants, planning all the fun things he wanted to do next, and making the most of his life a year later.

He never complained and continued to see the good in people and situations all the time. He took control of his circumstance rather than letting it control him. His positive, infectious outlook impacted everyone he met, so much so that I'm writing about him now.

When the cancer did eventually get the better of him, I was given the honor and privilege of speaking at his funeral. The church was overflowing; I don't think it had ever had so many people in it.

If Alex, battling the monster of terminal illness, was able to choose a positive attitude and impact the lives of so many around him, then there's no reason why the rest of us, operating most likely under less tragic circumstances, can't do the same.

Modeling Behavior

It's important for me to model to my kids maintaining a positive attitude.

I had the opportunity to do this one morning as I came into the kitchen dancing! Two of my children were sitting at the breakfast bar, looking a little tired, and my wife Diana was cooking. I came in dancing and singing and asked the children, "How are you guys?!" They replied with a grumble, "Daaaaaad." I pressed on: "Come on. It's going to be a really great day!" They started smiling immediately. I ran over and kissed them and made them feel like that day really *was* going to be great. I did this despite having had a very late night and feeling dreadful. I realized, however, that although I didn't feel great, I needed to get a handle on it. I could've gone into the kitchen with a bad attitude, but instead, because I made the children feel happy, I felt happy and my mood was raised. Had I chosen otherwise, the whole day could've been very different.

I often wonder why so many people keep a bad attitude for those who are closest to them and keep their best attitude for their colleagues at work?

The reality is, we need to be ever mindful of keeping our best attitude, to the best of our ability, with everyone we interact with. I probably don't need to tell you that attitudes are contagious; just as I model a positive attitude for my kids, we all model our attitudes for other people. Ulimately, you will create greater success for yourself (and a better community around you) the more you exhibit a positive attitude. Let's face it: no one wants to spend much time around someone whose attitude is a downer!

E + R = O

Author and motivational speaker Jack Canfield often references the equation E + R = O:

Event + Response = Outcome

Canfield explains that the *Events* of the world, E, are mostly things over which we have no control: the tsunami hits the shore, the cancer diagnosis comes in, the mile-wide tornado touches down.

To the extent we can influence *Outcomes*, O, the only thing we do have control over is the R in the formula, our *Response* to the event.

In Canfield's words, "If you don't like your "O"s, your Outcomes, than you have to change your "R"s, your response, because the "E" is just the way the world is... two plus two equals four. The two of the world isn't going to change. If you want five, you're going to have to do three."

Not many years ago, I had the occasion to create a rewarding outcome through my response to an unexpected event entirely out of my control. I was in America when the 2010 Icelandic volcano eruption cut off air travel to Europe for thousands of people. Away from my family, I suddenly faced an indefinite stay in Chicago.

But I shifted my attitude, put things into perspective, and decided to embrace the opportunity instead of bemoan it. I organized a series of lunches and dinners at some of Chicago's finest restaurants, promising myself that by the time I was able to return to the United Kingdom, I would have made some substantial progress with my businesses.

Team members back in the U.K. rose to the challenge, brilliantly managing the situation in my absence and demonstrating new skills. Meanwhile, in Chicago, my friends and I developed a business idea that subsequently went on to generate over $1 million in the following 12 months.

I eventually managed to get a flight home only five days later than planned and, apart from having been away from my family for nearly an extra week, getting stranded didn't feel so bad. Had I looked at the situation negatively and not embraced the opportunity, I would've squandered that time.

The other point I need to make here is that, because I have reached my Magic Number, being stranded in Chicago for five days did not incur the major financial strain it well could have. I did not have to sleep on the airport floor, like so many others did, nor count my dollars for my next meal. I was able to absorb the *event* (E) of a volcanic ash cloud over Europe with an easier and swifter *response* (R) because the means to cushion the blow were there. Had I been sleeping at the airport or scrounging for food for five days, arranging business lunches and hatching sales plans would have been the last thing on my mind, and the *outcome* (O) would have been quite different.

Attitude Activators

A positive attitude doesn't have to be reliant upon outside circumstances: a flight arriving on time, a good night's sleep, or having every untidy issue tied up by a certain period of time. A positive attitude can be a deliberate choice, a decision, regardless of what else is going on in your life. And to help make that choice, incorporating a daily talisman or ritual, what I call an Attitude Activator, can jolt you out of your preoccupation with your difficulties and into the present moment, the only place your problems will get resolved anyway.

I've broken down these Attitude Activators into two types: A daily Activator that sets you up for the day ahead, and an on-call Activator that can be used when you need it.

One of my favorite stories comes from Ash Prinjha, a man I've worked with for many years and who's now my financial coach—a key person in my community. With the most wonderful manner and disposition, Ash bounces into our office every morning, upbeat and with a smile.

Now, everyone has bad days once in a while—when we don't want to get out of bed, much less come into work. So one day, I had to pull him aside and ask what his secret was.

It's the archway, he tells me.

At that time, in our former location, we had an archway between the parking lot and entrance that you'd walk through to get to and from your car. Ash told me he stopped in that archway each morning before entering the office for what he called an "attitude trigger."

Ash would pause, take a deep breath, and choose to have a positive attitude for the day.

It was brilliant! I had to share this with the others in the office, who all loved the wisdom in it. We came to call it "Ash's Archway." Needless to say, from that point on, it was nearly impossible for any of us to walk through that archway without contemplating our own attitudes, and often adjusting them.

Right now, using the Magic Action below, I'd like you to decide on a trigger or something that happens in your morning routine that will serve as a reminder to approach the day with a great attitude. It could be a sign on your bedroom door, something you do on the way to work, or perhaps a note in your car with the words "dragon-slayer" on it—you choose!

Complete Magic Action #20 in your workbook: "Magic Attitude."

Magic Action

Now, let's look at an on-call Attitude Activator. When things haven't gone your way, but you still need to be on top of your game, it's important to put things into context and practice appreciation.

On occasion, when a situation runs afoul earlier in the day, but I still need to be in a meeting where I want to convey an especially positive or infectious attitude, I take some time to rapidly run through in my head all the great things I've done, all the successful meetings I've run in the past, and all the wonderful things that have happened in my life or are happening right now. I fill my mind with uplifting, positive thoughts—hopefully that have some relevance to that which I need the Attitude Activator for. I shift my mindset by putting the earlier mishap into a larger context and practicing appreciation for all that's transpired so far.

If you have a little more time, another great option is to simply engage in something that makes you happy: a conversation with a dear friend, a meal at your favorite restaurant, watching your favorite movie, or reading something funny—just something that raises your energy and makes you smile! It can be easy to shift your attitude simply by indulging in a little self-care.

Alternately, look over your "10 Magical Things About You" list or "What's Important to You?" answers in your workbook. See if doing so doesn't lift your mood, change your perspective, and shift your attitude in this very moment!

Magic Values

A central part of working the MAGIC Formula is ensuring that your behavior, actions, and decisions are congruent with your values—that your head and your heart are aligned.

Living an authentic life requires the principles of your heart and your actions out in the world (directed by your head) to be in sync. This may sound like a simplistic platitude, but it actually requires bravery and fortitude. When you think of the most admired people in history—Mahatma Gandhi, Abraham Lincoln, Martin Luther King, Jr., Nelson Mandela, and Joan of Arc, just to name a few—they all share demonstrated congruency between their personal values and actions in the world. And of course, there are so many other "ordinary" people who live truly authentic lives on a level that doesn't rise to international acclaim, but who enrich all of our existences as role models or through their contributions to society.

One example is my friend David. A manager of a five-star London hotel, he was hardworking and good at his job, so much so that a hotel guest offered him a job in Sweden—a very highly paid role in which he effectively doubled his income overnight.

Several years later, David and I were speaking, and he explained that after trying hard for some time in Sweden, he had decided to hand in his notice. He would leave his job and move to Barcelona. "Why?" I asked. He replied: "Because I want to work in a role where I am making a difference. I want to use my strengths, feel challenged, and work where the sun shines and the people are happy!"

He went on to explain that while he was earning a great income, he was just not satisfied in his role. Being challenged, making a difference, and using his strengths—together with the sunshine and happy people—is what truly motivated David. Because it came at the expense of what he valued most, David decided to take a pay cut to be where his heart and head better aligned.

Values play an important role throughout your life; if not sufficiently prioritized, they can substantially detract from your happiness.

For example, if you value family, but take very little vacation, work 70-hour weeks, and are never really present on weekends, you are operating in conflict. If you strive for success but fear rejection, life will be tough.

Values play an important role throughout your life; if not sufficiently prioritized, they can substantially detract from your happiness.

Understanding your values is also important when dealing with people. If you mix with people who have predominantly different values from your own, you're unlikely to respect them, and it can sometimes result in major conflict. One of my top values is integrity. So, if I'm with people who are not authentic, I pretty quickly begin to dislike them!

Your values do evolve over time. In my private consulting business, I often see people at the start of their careers define success as simply having money, being able to have nice holidays, and buying a great home. Then, if they decide to start a family, they define success less by material things and more about time with their children. Later in life, success is often equated with spending more time with grandchildren, pursuing a sport, or becoming more serious about a hobby.

Your Magic Number can work in the service of your values, not against them. Many people contend that aspiring towards financial independence requires compromising your ethics and integrity. I would like to assert the opposite. Money *can* be used to uphold your most valued principles and beliefs, both in the work in which you acquire it and in the way you use it afterwards. So, align your work, and how you perform it, with your values—you will tame, if not eliminate, the conflict between your heart and your head.

Use the following Magic Action to help you define and prioritize your values. Identify your top five and transfer them to your Magic Map, where you'll be able to reflect on them daily as you build a better, brighter, happier future.

Magic Action

Complete Magic Action #21 in your workbook: "Magic Values."

Magic Habits

Some people say they are not disciplined, but that's nonsense—they're actually just disciplined in bad habits! So, you need to learn the skill of replacing habits that hold you back with habits that move you forward. Because a habit is a behavior that, through repetition, becomes automatic, the key is applying repetition to the desired habit. There are many different opinions on how many repetitions it takes to make something a habit—it certainly varies from person to person—but we're going to use the "Rule of 21." This means it takes 21 days to establish a habit for something you do daily. There's no magic bullet here—it may take 30 or 45 days—you just need to do the thing with sufficient repetition that it becomes part of your subconscious behavior. You'll only learn what it takes for you by doing it. But think about it—even if you only adopted one great new habit every 90 days, this would equal four a year and 40 over a ten-year period. Can you imagine how different your life would be?

Of course, it's easier said than done. It does require effort. But if changing your life for the better was super easy, everybody would be doing it.

The only thing for certain is that time will go by—so the question is, what will you do in that time? A year from now, you'll be a year older, whether or not you replace any bad habits with good ones. Do you want your life to be the same then, or better?

Interestingly, many people think that to be successful in life you need to make big changes. The reality, however, as we discussed in Application, is that making big changes in life is very difficult. If you focus purely on making big changes, you will most likely set yourself up for failure, frustration, and disappointment. The best way to approach life is to get into the habit of making small changes and celebrating successes.

Remember, "80 percent of getting anything done is just getting started." So, get started with the habit of making small adjustments to improve your life and move toward your goals, and you'll see that change will happen.

Most of the time, when people fail to change a bad habit

Most of the time, when people fail to change a bad habit or adopt a new habit, it's because there are greater levels of negativity attached to the change than there are positive associations.

or adopt a new habit, it's because there are greater levels of negativity attached to the change than there are positive associations. Simply put, there must be more reasons *for* changing something than there are against it—otherwise, you just aren't going to follow through.

To help with this, choose a habit that will move you toward one or more of your goals. For example, if it is to become fitter and healthier, you'd want to replace a regular trip to your favorite coffee or fast-food place with a trip to the gym or long walk. If it involves buying something in the future you need to save for, it might be saving a certain amount of money each week to get there. If it is to learn a musical instrument, it might be to engage in some self-study for a specified amount of time each day. Remember, the key to adopting a new habit is repetition and consistency. The more great habits you can adopt and bad ones you can eliminate, the closer you'll move towards your goals and the life you desire.

Whether you choose the Magic Action below or use MagicFuture.com (the Magic Habits tool), we've made it easy for you to adopt a great new habit. Check off your progress day by day as you work to build a 21-day winning streak of empowering behaviors.

Magic Action

Complete Magic Action #22 in your workbook: "Magic Habits."

Now is a good time to mention that you should only adopt or replace one habit at a time. Like the rabbits, if you chase too many, you'll catch none; so don't overwhelm yourself. Five things left undone or unfinished are not as good as one thing done well. Whether you can successfully take on one, two, or three at a time will depend on your ability to consistently follow through. But it's best to begin with a small success and build on it.

But what about failure and setbacks? True, they cannot be ignored or avoided. Many people want to make positive change in their lives, but after a well-intended start, they weaken along the way and break the new routine: A smoker who'd quit has "just one" cigarette, a dieter has a cookie feast one night, a gym or practice session gets missed. The list goes on. It's very important to realize that *this is normal*. Most people need time, repetition, and consistency to get the results they desire—really, in most every endeavor. It is a very small minority who can pull off a perfect set of results, stick to a new routine, and—without a single mishap—reach their goal. They have laser-beam focus, unwavering resolve, and are to be applauded. But they are the minority.

The majority of us slip up from time to time. And here's where it gets interesting. For too many people, the slip-up is enough to break the resolution or routine and go back to their old ways, missing the pleasure they would get from making positive change in their lives. These folk often end up living lives, in the words of Thoreau, of quiet desperation.

A Word on Failure

A lot of us are, unfortunately, in a position where we have to deal with a lot of negative programming gathered over time. Our past experiences play a huge role in our mental state and how we deal with situations. If you come from a background where you've had quite a lot of negativity, it's very easy to slip into a destructive mentality.

However, fear of failure is only a good motivator when it prompts action. If it causes inaction or stagnation, it has no purpose. You need to reprogram yourself just as you would a computer virus—sort it out and start it all over again. There's a direct relationship between your past experiences and the decisions you make today.

I believe success cannot exist without failure. If you try anything hard in life, you will occasionally stumble and fall. The truly successful are those who get up time and time again. The unsuccessful are those who give up. The key—you have to keep trying. The more you try, the greater your levels of success will be.

If you can reframe failure as learning experiences that enable you to move forward to the next stage, you will appreciate how failure can lead to success. Michael Jordan captures this idea beautifully: "Our willingness to fail gives us the ability and opportunity to succeed where others may fear to tread. I've missed more than 9,000 shots in my career. I've lost almost 300 games. Twenty-six times, I've been trusted to take the game-winning shot and missed. I've failed over and over and over again in my life. And that is why I succeed."

Ask yourself, are you failing enough? Are you trying hard enough? Are you putting yourself in the position as often as possible where you can succeed or fail, or are you just in a routine where nothing is changing? Life's more fun when you take control and achieve more. Failure is often a key part of success.

So, GET BACK TO IT! Successful people learn from their blips, don't lose focus on their goals, and unsurprisingly, go on to achieve them.

Magic Hour

In the Application chapter, I mentioned that you'd be learning about your "Magic Hour." This is absolutely one of the best habits—perhaps *the* best—you'll ever acquire.

Thought leader Jim Rohn has said, "Never begin your day until it's finished on paper," and I have found that this habit has transformed the course of my day like no other. It's much easier to have a rewarding day if you can plan it before you start it.

I always seem to find myself busier than ever—juggling tasks, managing priorities, and meeting deadlines. So often, the busyness can just take over. When we lead crazy-busy lives, we can feel overwhelmed, stressed out, and anxious—and our quality and enjoyment of life deteriorates. A great way to manage the stress and strains of a busy life is to start the day with what I call your Magic Hour.

I get up a little earlier to do this—before the madness

starts! During *my* Magic Hour, I get myself into the right mindset with these three activities:

1. I think about three things in my life that I'm grateful for right now.
2. I take the opportunity to calmly review my long-range goals on my Magic Map.
3. I look at the day ahead and make a note of the three key things—yep, only three—I want to achieve from it.

By doing this, I start my day with a clear idea of what I want to accomplish, knowing that what I'm doing is aligned with my bigger picture and what's really important to me. So, try making your own Magic Hour the first new habit you adopt. As I mentioned, this was undoubtedly the best habit I've ever acquired. Invest this time, whether an actual hour or whatever you need, at the start of each day to express your gratitude, commit to your values, and decide what you are going to accomplish that day.

Complete Magic Action #23 in your workbook: "Magic Hour."

Magic Action

Magic Gratitude

Lastly, after all the sometimes hard work of adjusting your attitude, prioritizing your values, and reinforcing your habits, expressing gratitude is one of the most important things you can do. (Isn't it interesting that "great attitude" can be shortened to "gratitude"?)

Have you ever noticed what it's like to be around people who are really grateful for what they have? They tend to be nice people to be around, who exude warmth and happiness. They aren't usually moaning and complaining; they're just thoroughly pleasant company.

For me, gratitude is the foundation of attitude, values, and habits. There is so much we can all be grateful for. You can't have what you want until you want what you have, and the grounding you get from appreciating what's good in your life right now is very powerful.

Many years ago, I was encouraged by Dan Sullivan to start doing a "daily gratitude focus," when I would spend just a few minutes each morning listing five things I am truly grateful for in my life right now. (As you just learned, I now do this as part of my Magic Hour.) It could be something very straightforward, such as the weather being nice, my relationships, my colleagues, my friends, my employment, and my health. Taking five minutes to reflect on these five things, and writing them down, encourages the good things in your life to grow.

One thing I do with my children is ask them, over family mealtime, to share three things that worked out really well for them that day or that they're grateful for right now. It always lifts the mood and creates a very good feeling. And it reminds them that there are always many things each day to have gratitude for.

I refer to this as the "Gratitude Game." And this is a good exercise to do in many group settings. I go around the table one at a time and have each person tell me one thing they're grateful for. Often, when first asked, it's difficult for people to come up with three at once. However, when they hear about the good things going on with others in the group, invariably, everyone is able to come up with three. Taking turns creates enthusiasm and momentum as you go around the table. (Once you're used to doing it, it's easy to come up with three.)

Remember, when you're doing this with a group, don't be discouraged. You may find people are reluctant to join in at first. Nevertheless, persevere. The game shifts the energy in the room and changes everyone's mood and dynamic for the better. And I must confess that I do this exercise very selfishly, especially if I've had a challenging day. Hearing about others' positive experiences lifts my mood. I feed off the energy and enthusiasm that's created, and it puts me in a much better place.

Magic Action

Complete Magic Action #24 in your workbook: "Magic Gratitude."

* * * * *

It's quite interesting, isn't it, how much of this section on independence actually deals with how you interact with the rest of the world? It truly is your mindset—attitude, values, and gratitude, which all are reflected in how you get along with other people—that ultimately determines how much independence you'll enjoy in your life. Even among the habits you establish, the ones that are actions, there will be many only in your mind. (Positive thinking, while an attitude, is indeed a habit.) As Aristotle said, "We are what we repeatedly do. Excellence, then, is not an act, but a habit."

Very fitting, then, that we will wrap up the MAGIC Formula in the next section by examining *community*. Our independence impacts our community, and our community impacts our independence. It is a synergistic dynamic that can't be emphasized or developed one apart from the other. So, following your completion of the Round-Up on the next page, continue on to learn how to identify, contribute to, and grow the community around you.

ROUND-UP

- ❑ I have adopted an independence mindset.
- ❑ I take responsibility for my life and actions.
- ❑ I take control of my life, but without disregard for other people and the world around me.
- ❑ I maintain a positive attitude.
- ❑ I have created two Magic Attitude Activators: one that helps me start each day with a positive attitude and one that I can call on as needed.
- ❑ I maintain and express gratitude in my life, and I've played the Gratitude Game with family or friends.
- ❑ I have identified my top five values and make these a priority in my life.
- ❑ I commit to clarity about the habits in my life, and I understand changing them for the better is best done with small corrections, one habit at a time.
- ❑ I have incorporated the Magic Hour into my life.

C

Community

"In all our searching, the only thing we've found that makes the emptiness bearable is each other."
CARL SAGAN, *Contact*

WHILE INDEPENDENCE IS INCREDIBLY REWARDING, we need the help of others to fulfill our potential, achieve our goals, and make measurable progress in reasonable time. This is the "C" that concludes my formula.

The famous psychologist Abraham Maslow is best known for defining human needs and their priorities in our lives. His seminal work, *Maslow's Hierarchy of Needs,* details how foundational needs must be met before higher needs can be addressed. The first three are not surprising: basic survival, safety, and security. But interestingly, the next two are belonging and socialization; in other words, we need to be part of a *community.* The two higher needs, esteem (to do with one's ego) and self-actualization (discovering true meaning), cannot be met without community. Too often, though, we seek to develop our esteem and find higher purpose in our lives without stopping to seriously consider whether we have a supportive community around us.

It's not a coincidence that all of the successful people I have worked with appreciate the importance and power of the contribution of others. They actively seek to surround themselves with the right communities and teams. Having the right people around you will transform your results and happiness, and ultimately your life.

Having the right people around you will transform your results and happiness, and ultimately your life.

Conversely, spending time with people who drain your energy, try to pull you away from your goals, or criticize you in an unconstructive way will only undermine your efforts and satisfaction with life. Fortunately, you get to decide with whom you associate. It can be very hard to cut away these people, especially if they've been in your life for a long time, but you must, if you want a better shot at reaching your goals. At the very least, you need to limit your experience with them to situations or conversations that are positive and enjoyable. If that's not at all possible, I can't emphasize enough the importance of letting them go, particularly so you can make room for people who better fit your needs.

I've mentioned in this book my travels to Chicago and Arizona several times a year as part of two coaching and networking groups, both of which comprise growth-oriented entrepreneurs. Many of them have become personal friends. Outside of these people, there are also many others who have been kind enough to provide me with advice, guidance, and mentoring over the past 25 years. And of course, there are those in my family, business network, colleagues, and friends without whom my life would be very different. There are too many to list here, of course, but I am grateful to each and every one of them. When I reflect on my life so far, I can without question attribute a tremendous amount of my success to these people. In ways both big and small, each has played a role, and all have come together to be this grand experience I know as my life! We simply cannot go far on our own.

Of course, a lifetime is a long time (hopefully!), so you can't expect your community to be static—it will evolve as you grow, changing with your interests, needs, and pursuits. But no matter how much or how often your community changes, you should always respect those in it with full gratitude. Perhaps nowhere in your life is gratitude more impactful and meaningful than in your community.

So, in these following pages, I am going to show you how to:

- Identify your community
- Contribute and add value to your community
- Expand your community
- Find and work with a mentor
- And recruit a "goals buddy" for accountability

Now, let's get going!

Identifying Your Community

The first step to a stronger community is determining who makes up yours at the moment.

The dictionary defines *community* as:

"a social, religious, occupational, or other group sharing common characteristics or interests and perceived or perceiving itself as distinct in some respect from the larger society within which it exists."

For our purposes here, let's divide yours into three groups:

Your physical community—People you have physically met or continue to meet and spend time with, such as family, friends, colleagues, associates, and the guy at Starbucks who knows exactly how you like your latté.

Your virtual community—Those whom you've met and interact with via the Internet or technology, such as social-media contacts, online forum friends, and online group members. Naturally, these people can overlap those in your physical community or go back and forth between the two. But regardless, your virtual community will comprise far greater numbers of people with far greater reach, which makes it vital to tap into.

Your potential community—This might seem odd at first, but I think it's good to be forward-thinking and, therefore, to have an idea who you'd *like to have* in your community. These typically are people whose company you would enjoy or whose inclusion in your community would be relevant and helpful to your goals.

You've probably heard the adage, "If you don't know what you're looking for, you're unlikely to ever find it." I'll modify this to say, *if you don't know what you're looking for, no one in your circle can help you find it.* So, as you cultivate your communities, both existing and potential, view everyone through the lens of your goals. Will this person help me get closer to or farther away from my goals? But remember, when I say "goals" I do include those that are personally fulfilling. You may have a close friend in your life whose best attribute is giving you a good laugh right when you need it most; she may not do anything for your career, but she sure makes life more enjoyable. This reminds me of something brilliant the great Tom Hopkins wrote in his book *The Official Guide to Success*: "Sometimes the most important thing you could be doing right now is nothing." In other words, when looking at how your community members support your life, remember life is a balance of what you do and what you don't.

Magic Action

Complete Magic Action #25 in your workbook: "Magic Community."

Contributing Value to Your Communities

Now, I want you to ask yourself, *Do my people know why I appreciate them?* If the answer is no, you may want to let them know—in the right way and at the right time. We all like to feel valued, and I see all too often that people don't tell others why they value them, which is crazy really.

You may be familiar with the saying, "The more you give, the more you get." Along those lines, I'd like you to now write down how you could provide something of value to each of the people you've listed. Think really hard about this. What could you help them achieve? What could you share with them? What could you do to make their lives easier? Next, write down how *they* could add value to *you*. And finally, list some specific action steps that could be taken to achieve both added-value potentials (yours to theirs and theirs to yours). Use the exercise on the opposite page to note your answers.

To expand on this, let's say there's someone in your community you could help, but you haven't told the person. A great way to step forward would be to take him out for a meal—explain that you've spent some time thinking about the important people in your community who truly make a difference in your life and your progress, and that he is one of them. Use the opportunity to express your appreciation for him and let him know, as a way of demonstrating your gratitude, you'd like to help in some way. You could talk about the things you had come up with prior to the meal, but be sure to ask if there are any other ways you could help. Focus on contributing to him *first* and, in time, you'll find ample opportunity to receive his help in your goals. This may seem manipulative, but it's really not. It's just a proactive way of doing what you naturally and unconsciously do with the people closest to you, ultimately creating greater opportunities for *win-win* arrangements throughout your communities.

We all like to feel valued, and I see all too often that people don't tell others why they value them, which is crazy really.

As I mentioned, your community is guaranteed to change over time, so it's smart to repeat this exercise every three months. Though it's simple, you will be amazed by the good will and benefits that come from it.

Growing Your Community

The most organic way to grow your community is to get engaged with things that excite you and connect with people who share your interests. An obvious example would be joining a gym if you're looking to get fit. But go beyond the obvious. It's interesting to me how many people show up at the gym and work out in isolation. Instead, recognize it as an opportunity; you are surrounded with like-minded people with a common goal. You can learn from them, use them to stay motivated, and do the same in return—and perhaps even connect in some way beyond fitness.

No matter your interests, there are certainly groups out there to explore, and the Internet has become the best way to track these down. I'd be surprised if you couldn't find one related to your passion, but if not, consider starting such a group through MeetUp.com. You may just discover an untapped shared interest with other people who've also been seeking such a group. Likewise, social-media sites such as Facebook and Google+ are full of communities on nearly every subject imaginable. Join, and then tune in for a while before contributing—your goal is to add value, so you'll be learn what this can be if you spend time "listening" first. I also think it's ideal, if you can, to contribute in some meaningful way a few times *before* asking others to assist you. This builds better rapport in the long run.

Ultimately, with all the real world and online options available to us these days, there truly is no valid excuse for not growing your community.

Bringing It Together

Successful people are often like the conductors of an orchestra—they lead the performance but have people around them to help make the music a reality. This is a great way to think of your community. It's yours, and as the conductor, it's your responsibility to coordinate your community in order to make the music you want.

The best and brightest entrepreneurs I've known all identified their own unique abilities at some point—then surrounded themselves with a highly competent team of people who complement their skill set. I've yet to meet someone who gets everything done without any help. Occasionally, however, I do meet people who *think* they can!

Successful people are often like the conductors of an orchestra—they lead the performance but have people around them that help make the music a reality.

For all the benefits of communities, though, there are some aspects to be warned about. Here are two to keep in mind:

1. There are people who spend so much of their time absorbed in their community that they don't get enough of the "application" in MAGIC done. I've been known once or twice to suggest to my children that, while I think Facebook is wonderful, they should devote a little less time to screen-sucking!
2. Technology has made it possible to communicate virtually, and this ability is only increasing in ease. So, we should be very careful to remember the value and power that comes from in-person interaction. Much of the best of life still happens when we're face to face.

Your Magic Mentor

The dictionary defines a *mentor* as:

"a wise and trusted counselor or teacher; an influential senior sponsor or supporter."

In many progressive businesses, especially professional service firms, it's quite common to have a culture of mentoring or sponsoring younger up-and-coming stars in the firm. If you are fortunate enough to be in an environment where mentoring is encouraged, wonderful. Make the best of it as long as you can. But if you're not, now is the time to be proactive and get a mentor of your own.

One of the things I look back on—that's made me very,

very fortunate—is that I grew up without a father at home. At the time it sucked, let me tell you! When my parents split up, I was nine, and I was not very happy about it. You don't always see the silver lining in the cloud in the moment, especially at that age—so I truly hated it when my father left. It was a desperate time, and I was very sad. With hindsight, however, it was probably one of the best things that ever happened to me. My mother was, and still is, a wonderful source of support and love—but my father leaving meant that, from a very young age, I started seeking out advice from others. It's something I've done ever since.

Years later, when I first started work, the manager of my department impressed me. He was a gruff man, highly organized, and came across to me as very powerful. He was looking after a team of a hundred people and, without my realizing it at the time, he actually took a shine to me because I was eager to improve myself. He ended up mentoring me. With his valuable guidance, I ended up becoming one of the youngest managers in the history of the business—at the age of nineteen, I had a department of fifteen people (all older than I was!) reporting to me. This had come about because I was willing to embrace change, willing to listen, willing to learn, and I had someone who was there to teach me. He was my first mentor, but by no means my last.

Since then, I've been fortunate to benefit from the input of various mentors and coaches over the years and have ended up with a team of them I highly trust and respect. They each have their own unique abilities and areas where they help me with my thinking, and they always support me in the challenges I face as I continue my journey.

From this experience, I've learned there is one essential element to a successful mentoring/coaching relationship:

You must be willing to learn and listen.

Please don't mentally skip over this point! It's easy to brush past as being obvious, but too many times mentees want help without being willing to possibly *change* in order to implement the mentor's guidance. And when this is the case, the process won't work and the arrangement will be a waste of time for both of you. Furthermore, it's so much easier to approach and gain a mentor when you've applied the MAGIC Formula to your life. Here's why.

Somebody who has lots of motivation, is getting ahead, applying herself, and has a growth and independence mindset is *exactly* the type of person a mentor wants to help—someone who will embrace every bit of learning and advice and use it. It's not a very attractive proposition for a mentor to support somebody who hasn't clarified her goals, hasn't built a plan to accomplish them, and doesn't appear motivated and ready to take the action required. As a mentor, why would you bother spending time with someone who lacks vision, clarity, and purpose? Bluntly put, it would just be a waste of your time.

Too many times mentees want help without being willing to possibly *change* in order to implement the mentor's guidance.

On the other hand, as the mentee, if you know where you're heading and are eager to share your goals and plans, this is energizing for a mentor, who may see an earlier version of himself in you. A mentor's role is to provide you with the benefit of his experience and wisdom to help you achieve what you want. Perhaps most important, a great mentor will help you *discover* answers rather than just provide them.

And now that you know the mindset and position you must be in to successfully approach prospective mentors, let's look at finding them.

Typically, they will be known to you because of their history and their skill set. You'll either have an existing personal connection or you'll be aware of them through the media, your profession, or where you live—it may even be someone in one of your communities. It could be that you aspire to be like your mentor, or it could be your mentor has achieved something you want to achieve as well. It's important, however, that your mentor prospects have the expertise to be able to help you make smarter decisions and accelerate your progress. It's not good enough for someone to simply be willing and available.

Now, you may be wondering at this point whether it's okay to have more than one at a time. It certainly is, but be careful. They have to complement one another or you could find yourself getting very confused by conflicting advice or guidance. As with most things in life, there are usually multiple ways to get what you want, and you can't have two different mentors directing you down two different paths toward the same goal. For this reason, having multiple mentors usually works best when they are guiding you in distinct areas of your development—you may have a financial mentor (as I do) helping you build wealth, a business mentor supporting the growth of your company, and a health mentor enhancing your physical fitness.

Mentors aren't there to *tell you* what to do; they help you *discover* the solutions to your problems or provide additional perspective on a situation based on their experiences.

Another point of potential confusion occurs when mentees receive advice they don't agree with. It's fair and reasonable that you won't take 100% of the advice a mentor gives you, and he or she will understand this. Besides, as I mentioned before, mentors aren't there to *tell you* what to do; they help you *discover* the solutions to your problems or provide additional perspective on a situation based on their experiences. It's this additional perspective that can be invaluable in helping you come up with a strategy, game plan, or solution. Ultimately, you decide your course, whether following or against your mentor's advice.

It's worth noting at this point that mentoring relationships work best when there's a common connection between the mentor and the mentee outside of the main subject area. It could be that you both share an interest in the same type of sport, dining, wine, music, cars, hobbies, etc. This gives you something that you're both passionate about and can talk about outside the primary purpose of the mentorship, which builds a broader bond and mutual value. So, as you develop a target list, keep this in mind.

Being prepared is key when approaching a prospective mentor. So, here is a basic list of items to provide him or her:

- Some background on your experience
- Why you're seeking a mentor
- What your objectives are for the future
- Why you think he/she is the right mentor for you
- Some idea of the amount of time you would be expecting

On this last point, I recommend initially keeping this low—maybe one or two hours per quarter. Then, if the relationship develops and there's value in more regular contact, the time will grow naturally.

It may take a while, but if you follow the advice in this section, don't give up, and always maintain a positive and respectful attitude, you will eventually find a mentor. And when you do, congratulations! It will be a turning point in your life, one you will always remember. But of course, that's only the beginning, so here are some further bits of advice on keeping the relationship productive (for both of you):

- Don't waste you mentor's time—be punctual for your appointments, and be prepared.
- Provide succinct updates on your progress via whatever way she or he prefers.
- Be courteous, polite, and respectful at all times; err on the side of being more formal unless told otherwise.
- Express appreciation for his/her advice and especially time—for many mentors, time is what they always have little of.
- Arrange to meet with your mentor on a periodic, agreed-upon basis.
- Be clear on the areas where you'd like help and communicate them in advance of the time you have together.
- Be entirely open and honest. Don't withhold information, even though it may be embarrassing (such as your mistakes). Otherwise, without all the relevant details, it'll be difficult for the person to provide much useful help, or

worse, she may give you inadvertently bad advice.

Finally, accept the reality that mentors normally have a shelf life. As you develop and grow, it's possible you will find yourself outgrowing your current mentor and be ready to move on. Acknowledge this likelihood at the beginning of the relationship—you should only both continue as long as the mentor is comfortable spending time with you and you are getting tremendous value.

Now that we've covered the various aspects of mentorship, the following Magic Action will help you find a great mentor. It even includes a sample letter or email you can use when contacting prospects.

Complete Magic Action #26 in your workbook: "Magic Mentor."

Your Goals Buddy

In the work environment, people are normally accountable to a person or group of people, which is naturally helpful in making things happen. However, when setting out to improve an aspect of our lives or achieve something we've wanted for a long time, we are seldom accountable to anyone other than ourselves—as a result, many of us have great intentions that fall by the wayside. Being our own "judge and jury," we can either let ourselves off the hook too easily or condemn ourselves as not worthy of our goals.

To battle this natural tendency, share your important goals with a trusted person who can be your "goal buddy"—introducing some accountability in the same way people have in the workplace. Great business people and athletes have individual coaches because it enhances their performance, and that's exactly what a goal buddy can do for you.

It's a great feeling to have the satisfaction of reporting to this person that you've achieved what you set out to do. Conversely, your buddy can also give you a bit of a nudge if you're not doing what you said you would or if you're starting to fall behind.

Undoubtedly, as you work to achieve certain goals, you may face some rough spots. Being able to talk to somebody who will be supportive, encouraging, and sincerely interested in your achievement is hugely helpful, if not entirely necessary—"a problem shared is a problem halved." So, the ideal person filling this role will be someone who cares about you and your well-being enough to make the effort to help you stay on track in good times and bad. In fact, it's quite common for this person to get infected with your purpose and vision and end up motivated to set bigger goals for his or her own life! (And of course, you can be a goal buddy for your goal buddy.)

Lastly, Facebook, Google+, LinkedIn, and the like can be great accountability tools. If you're someone who takes pride in doing what you say, then posting your goals on your social network might just be an ideal way to keep yourself on track. Additionally, consider setting up a goal-buddy circle of multiple people, in which you can create a buzz and help spur each other on. A little accountability goes a long way!

Magic Action

Complete Magic Action #27 in your workbook: "Goal Buddies."

* * * * *

"I alone cannot change the world, but I can cast a stone across the waters to create many ripples." Those words, from Mother Teresa, perfectly reflect the relationship between independence and community. While we all strive for—and are possibly genetically programmed for—autonomy, we are ultimately unable to accomplish much with our lives without the involvement of others. Moreover, as Maslow prescribed in his hierarchy of needs, we will be profoundly dissatisfied and unhappy attempting to navigate the world on our own. Remember, the plight of the man played by Tom Hanks in *Cast Away*—he was ultimately willing to risk his life to escape the island rather than face what seemed to be a future of utter solitude.

So, as you strike out on your journey toward reaching your Magic Number, remember that it will never be reached at the expense of community. What you deliver to your community, in the service of others, will come back to you in return. It's a symbiotic relationship. As many wise women and men have said, "You can best achieve your goals through helping other people achieve theirs."

ROUND-UP

- ❑ I understand that I have multiple communities in my life and they aren't static.
- ❑ I have identified my communities, both physical and virtual.
- ❑ I have listed my top-five people in each community.
- ❑ I commit to contributing and adding value to my communities.
- ❑ I commit to expanding my communities and have identified ways to do that, as well as people I'd like included.
- ❑ I appreciate the value of mentoring and coaching, and I commit to finding a compatible one and developing a good process for this in my life.
- ❑ I have a goals buddy and/or a magic team who will provide support and accountability in my life.

Conclusion

"I went to the woods because I wished to live deliberately, to front only the essential facts of life, and see if I could not learn what it had to teach, and not, when I came to die, discover that I had not lived."

HENRY DAVID THOREAU

THOREAU'S WORDS RING THROUGH THE YEARS from the time they were written around 1846. For millennia, humanity's wizards and witches, artists and mystics "went to the woods"; they receded into seclusion to discover the meaning and magic of life. Artists hole up in nature cabins, monks cloister themselves in monasteries, and sages retreat to mountain caverns, each to learn what life has to teach and front the "essential facts" of it.

But what if you don't want to seclude yourself? What if you don't want to retreat to the mountaintops, run off to a monastery, or isolate yourself in a forest cabin? What if you want to stay right where you are, smack dab in the noisy, distraction-filled, modern-day life and still explore the magic and meaning of it all—to still live deliberately?

What then?

Well, then, different tactics are in order.

Weaving magic into human life does not mean you have to seclude yourself in isolation and command invisible forces. It just means you have to command yourself.

In the preceding chapters, I hope you have learned that living a conscious, deliberate, even magical existence is not a mystery. What it requires is self-mastery. And I hope you'll embrace the strategies to embark on that mastery with my MAGIC Formula.

Taking control, achieving more, and loving life requires a little discipline, some resilience, self-resolve, and an open mind, but no actual magic.

And if I, lentil boy, can go from sitting forlorn and bike-less at the BMX park to where I am today, you can achieve great things too.

So, get to it!

Remember that all progress starts with telling the truth, so build your motivation by spending some time thinking about what's really important to you. Ask yourself your unique question and go to MagicFuture.com to discover your Magic Number. Then use the site's Magic Vision tool to construct your vision board, and keep it in front of you on your smartphone, tablet, computer, and wall.

If I, lentil boy, can go from sitting forlorn and bike-less at the BMX park to where I am today, you can achieve great things too.

Once you're fired up, don't let that flame fizzle. If you haven't already, fill out your Magic Map. Remember the tugboat: weighted silk string, then rope, then chain. Type in your three-year, one-year, and 90-day goals, and focus on your big tasks first—the rocks—before you grapple with the smaller, less relevant tasks—the pebbles and sand.

And don't let your newfound motivation die with pretty pictures on the wall. Apply, apply, apply your new strategies. Keep your plans flexible, follow through, and no beating yourself up.

Be committed to growth, both on a day-to-day and longer-term, proactive basis. Use weekly, quarterly, and annual reviews to plan forward and measure backward, and take the time to celebrate your successes, even the little ones. Stay self-aware, stay coachable, and concentrate on your unique ability.

Aspire towards independence. The concept might seem clichéd and worn, but it is only through independence, financial and otherwise, that we are truly able to live a deliberate life and carve the path for ourselves we see fit. Keep a great attitude, exhibit and express gratitude, keep your values in front of mind, and foster great habits. In the meantime, don't let slip-ups break your resolve and remember to incorporate the Magic Hour as your first new habit of the day.

"Don't be satisfied with stories, how things have gone with others. Unfold your own myth."
-*Rumi*, Essential Rumi

Lastly, and always, focus on community. No one is an island and—I would add—no one would want to be. Having people to share in your successes and failures is key to a happy, fulfilled life, so never let the hot pursuit of goals and achievements come at the dire expense of friends, family, and colleagues who care for and support you and whom you support and care about.

By that same token, those who do *not* support or care about you do *not* deserve your time, and they may sometimes be difficult to discern. Constructive criticism and alternate perspectives are welcome and necessary, but if you find yourself repeatedly among people who drain your energy, mock your convictions, or disparage your plans, walk away quickly. They do so usually because *they* have tried but given up, and mostly because they are too afraid to try.

So, identify your communities—physical, virtual, and potential—and see what you can do to expand and contribute to them. Clarify your objectives and seek out a wise and trusted mentor to guide you. Moreover, don't let your motivation falter because your burdens are too heavy or there's no one looking over your shoulder to make you complete your tasks. Remember that a problem shared is a problem halved, so find a goals buddy to lighten your load, spur you on, and keep you accountable. In the end, we're all in this together.

So, slay those dragons. Move those mountains. And work the MAGIC Formula for all it's worth:

Motivation—Find out what moves you;

Application—Move ceaselessly in that direction;

Growth—Learn from that movement, rigorously explore hindsight, and be vigilant about lifelong education;

Independence—Achieve the freedom to which we all aspire, the ability to control and direct the course of your own life;

Community—Foster the sweetness of life: the people who accompany you on your path, provide comfort during your failures, and cheer on your successes... ultimately, what makes it all worthwhile.

Now, you may recall in the introduction that I would have you re-take the Happiness Test after we'd gone through the MAGIC Formula. I'd like you to stop and do that now for the Magic Action below. See how your results compare with your first results in Magic Action #2. And be sure to repeat the test every 90 days to measure your progress.

Complete Magic Action #28 in your workbook: "The Magical Happiness Test."

> "If a man moves confidently in the direction of his dreams, and endeavors to live the life he has imagined, he will know a success unexpected in common hours."
>
> THOREAU

So, as you see, there are no spectacular spells, no secret potions, and no crystal balls. Still, that doesn't mean your efforts will be absent unexplained, fortuitous, and unexpected circumstances. In the renowned words of W.H. Murray, in his book, *The Scottish Himalaya Expedition*:

> Until one is committed, there is hesitancy, the chance to draw back—Concerning all acts of initiative (and creation), there is one elementary truth that ignorance of which kills countless ideas and splendid plans: that the moment one definitely commits oneself, then Providence moves too. A whole stream of events issues from the decision, raising in one's favor all manner of unforeseen incidents, meetings and material assistance, which no man could have dreamt would have come his way.

So, in essence, you'll have real magic—the mystical kind—at your aid as well. No one really knows the extent that chance or choice play in a human being's existence, but we have to behave as if the choice is ours, and let Providence move as it may.

The spinner of contemporary magical tales, J.K. Rowling, the author of the *Harry Potter* series, had this to say on the matter at Harvard's commencement address in 2008: "There is an expiry date on blaming your parents for steering you in the wrong direction; the moment you are old enough to take the wheel, responsibility lies with you."

And she would know. Rowling went from being on welfare and, as she puts it, "jobless, a lone parent, and as poor as it is possible to be in modern Britain, without being homeless," to a life as a writer—her lifelong dream—and, as a consequence, one of the richest women in the world.

But is she a wild exception? An outlier? A fluke?

When my father left my mother, sister, and me when I was nine, and I watched my mother work night and day to keep food on the table, I'm not sure I could have envisioned my life today, having reached my Magic Number—achieving the point where work is optional—and jetting across the ocean every couple of months to learn and grow.

Yet, here I am.

And these previous two examples are not the only cases in point. There are others:

Christopher Gardner is a wealthy stockbroker and fund

manager who started life out with a physically abusive stepdad. As Gardner writes in his book, *Start Where You Are*, his mother's husband "took pleasure in letting me know that he wasn't my daddy either—sometimes at the end of a shotgun barrel."

Later, as a single dad, Gardner and his toddler son stayed in homeless shelters and subway bathrooms at night while he learned his trade at a competitive internship at Dean Witter. From these tumultuous beginnings, Gardner went on to form his own brokerage firm, Gardner Rich, and later sold a minority stake in the company for millions of dollars. His take on the subject:

> Was I a fluke? Was I one of the lucky few to ever break out of the rut? Not by a long shot. There are folks everywhere in every walk of life who are defying statistics every single day. Far too few awards are being given to the millions across the country and around the world, and in every community, who are succeeding in parenthood and personhood. Not in spite of the odds, but sometimes because of them! Of everyone I've met who grew up in the bleakest of conditions to become the opposite of all our surroundings, challenges, and issues—all of us who could have easily become that which was right in our faces—I have never met anyone who was a fluke. The power of choice, not chance, was what made the difference.

Academy Award-nominated actor Will Smith portrayed Gardner in the story of his life in the 2006 film, *The Pursuit of Happyness*. Gardner now speaks to audiences around the globe and raises investment capital for ventures in South Africa.

So, you are in good company, and you are not alone. You owe it to yourself; you owe it to those who came before you. Get to it.

Test your limits, check your ceiling, and be the flea that

jumps out of the jar. Happiness and a well-lived life are worthy pursuits not only for their own sakes; they influence all those around you, and sometimes even those *not* so close around you—as I hope this book has, as I hope my MAGIC Formula has. So, slay those dragons and move those mountains, and when you do, tell me about it at StefanWissenbach.com.

J.K. Rowling, the creator of Hogwarts and Hagrid and Horcruxes and Hufflepuff, put it this way: "We don't need magic to transform our world. We carry all the power we need inside ourselves already. We have the power to imagine better."

And, I would add, don't just imagine—do it.

I'll be cheering you on.

Acknowledgements

THE FACT THAT I HAVE BEEN ABLE to write this book is down to the wonderful people that have been in, and are in, my life—my community. I thank you all with all my heart; you have changed my world. This is my first book, and therefore an ideal opportunity to say "thank you" and recognize those who are special to me.

To my fabulous wife, Diana: The words "thank you" don't express my gratitude sufficiently. You have been a constant source of love, support, and encouragement. From the day we met you have believed in me and you inspire me to reach higher. I love you, your company, and our journey! This is our time.

Oli, Alex, and Max, you're amazing. Watching you grow up is one of the best experiences of my life and you continue to make me proud. Reach for the stars!

Mum, you are such an inspiration. Your approach to life has taught me so much. The sacrifices you made as a single parent to bring up Kate and me remain appreciated to this day. I now smile as I remember you throwing away the television so we would read books. And, by the way, I love lentils!

Kate, thank you for putting up with me. We have the bond that great siblings have, and you have a special place in my heart.

Moley, thanks for introducing me to so many different things and for being such a great adopted father. I enjoy your company tremendously. Thank goodness I had a chance to grow up before you met Mum!

I am blessed to have a wonderful family, both immediate and extended, and thank you all for your love and support.

Jayne, I really appreciate your relentless support and dedication. You have been the perfect assistant through some of the most challenging times in my life. You connect the dots like no one I know. Thank you for making me look good. You are a superstar.

Ash Prinjha, my wingman. And here we are. What a journey. The next phase will be even better!

Hayley Goode, your loyalty and commitment are second to none. We've seen much change together, and I love your insatiable desire to explore new possibilities. Thank you.

Richard Greenhalgh, thank you for your dedication and support in such a key phase of Magic Future's growth. You made a difference, and I appreciate your contribution.

Todd Brook and the team at EIM, you've brilliantly executed my vision like no other agency has ever managed to do. Thank you.

To all of the rest of my business community, I am grateful for your unique abilities, friendships, and contributions. You make business fun!

To all the Magic Future users who continue, by the day, to complete actions, achieve goals, and fulfill your potential: thank you. You have no idea how your success makes me feel and how it inspires me to make Magic Future better and better, as well as available to as wide an audience as possible.

Dan Sullivan, you are a brilliant visionary and were the first person to have a bigger vision for Magic Future than its founder. Your belief and support has been a huge contributor to what's been achieved. I am blessed to have you and

Babs as friends. I look forward to celebrating the achievement of your vision for Magic Future—soon!

To the team at Strategic Coach, I'm so grateful for everything you do. I hope you appreciate that what you deliver changes lives!

To my former coaches and mentors—Dave Larue, Peter Haddon, Chris Watson, and Mike Wilson: You are extraordinary gentlemen, and I appreciate your wisdom and guidance. It made a difference.

David Bellamy: Our actions define us. The day you stood by me in 2000 will forever be remembered. Thank you.

Craig McAree: It takes courage to back and support an idea. Thank you for being the visionary at Ernst & Young who took a risk on me and my vision. Thank you, Liz Bingham and Patricia McEvoy, for also believing and making the decision that Ernst & Young would be the first professional services firm to provide Magic Future as a corporate benefit. You took a risk and the world rewards risk-takers. Your support has helped me accelerate getting Magic Future out in the world. More people will have their lives impacted by Magic because you showed courage and adopted a new innovation.

Lee Noble and the term at Sterling, thank you for support Magic Future in the early days.

Graham Defries: Thank you for all you do for Magic Future and for making our Foundation a reality.

Thank you to all my friends who have supported my idea for a bigger and brighter future for the many rather than the few: Peter Hatherly, Jon Little, Stuart Layzell, Stuart Knight, Bill and Sue Auden, Neal and Roger Kutner, Anita Prinjha, Richard Greenhalgh, Todd Brook, Jade Thamasucharit, Jonny Aucamp, Mike Shirley, Rob Brophy, Danny Langley, Phil Hylander, Adrian Guldener, and Mike Greenberg. I am grateful that you followed your hearts and heads and backed me. I appreciate your believing in me. Thank you, too, to the other Magic Future investors—this is an investment that works!

Patsy Rodenburg: We discussed this book at length

before it was written and you gave me so much confidence. Thank you for your wisdom and advice. It's my voice!

Andrew Chapman and Mona Kuljurgis: Thank you. This book would not have happened without you. You exceeded my expectations by some margin and added so much value! I will sing your praises for many years to come.

Finally, thank you to YOU, the reader. Unless you're one of the people named above, you're either thinking you should be or you're just very good at finishing things. If it's the latter, you've done fabulously well to get this far. If I missed you out, I'm sorry.

Either way, it's time to put the book down now. Please go and make some MAGIC!

About the Author

STEFAN WISSENBACH is a successful entrepreneur, author, speaker, strategic advisor, and philanthropist.

From a humble but happy childhood, Stefan has built several successful business and is an advisor to a number of leading business figures and accomplished entrepreneurs. He is passionate about providing education and inspiration to enable others to fulfill their potential and bridge the gap between aspiration and achievement. His unique approach is to simplify the complex and provide a framework for people to take action, distilling a lifetime of learning into simple success strategies that anyone can master.

Stefan is the founder of The Wissenbach Group, a U.K.-based strategic advisory firm working with a small number of private clients; creator of Magic Number; the visionary and founder behind MagicFuture.com; and co-founder of The Magic Future Foundation. His website is StefanWissenbach.com, and his Twitter handle is @SWissenbach.

He is married with three children and lives in Warwickshire, England.

Order Copies of This Book

Slaying Dragons and Moving Mountains is available for special sales and bulk purchases to use as a premium or incentive—customer/client appreciation or acquisition; employee retention, motivation, or training; donor appreciation; and other benefit purposes. To receive information on this program, contact us at Inquiries@StefanWissenbach.com.

Made in the USA
Monee, IL
04 November 2026

67385953R10075